Self-Esteem

Tools
For
Recovery

Lindsey Hall & Leigh Cohn

gürze books

Self-Esteem Tools for Recovery

Gürze Books
P.O. Box 2238
Carlsbad, CA 92018
(619)434-7533

Cover design by Abacus Graphics, Carlsbad, CA

Library of Congress Cataloging-in-Publication Data

Hall, Lindsey, 1949-
   Self-esteem tools for recovery.

   Bibliograpy: p.
   1. Self-respect.   2. Psychotherapy.   3. Self-care,
Health. I. Cohn, Leigh. II. Title.
RC489.S43H35   1989   158'.1   89-11852
ISBN 0-936077-08-5

NOTE:

The authors and publisher of this book intend for this publication to provide accurate information. It is sold with the understanding that it is meant to complement, not substitute for, professional medical and/or psychological services.

6 8 0 9 7

Table of Contents

Introduction   v

Tool 1:   What's your problem?!   7

Tool 2:   Your problem has served you well.   12

Tool 3:   It takes courage to heal.   18

Tool 4:   Our secrets keep us separate.   23

Tool 5:   It's your recovery.   28

Tool 6:   Recovery begins when you're ready.   34

Tool 7:   Recovery is an on-going process.   40

Tool 8:   Whatever you do matters.   45

Tool 9:   Who are you?   50

Tool 10: Know where are you going
          and how to get there.   55

Tool 11: You have to add something
          if you're taking something away.   61

Tool 12: Don't be afraid of mistakes.   66

Tool 13: Acceptance transcends control.   72

Tool 14: Feelings: Are we having fun yet?   82

Tool 15: Think and speak positively.   89

Tool 16: Face the truth about your family.   95

Tool 17: Be aware of the media's message.   103

Tool 18: Keep good company.   110

Tool 19: Practice love.   114

Tool 20: Expect miracles.   120

Notes   124

Introduction

Self-esteem is both the means to recovery and it is the goal. No matter what kind of problem you have, self-esteem will assist you in the process of living life more fully, without artificial stimuli, coping mechanisms, and habitual behavior. It will help you find guidance, acceptance, confidence, and love inside of yourself, now and always.

Here are twenty self-esteem tools to practice. Each tool develops one main idea and is complete by itself. Some have inspirational stories, and others challenge you to examine your beliefs in different ways. Many have practical, specific tasks to help you apply these ideas to your daily life. Every tool includes an exercise which invites your active participation. Get the most from the tools by reading one, doing the exercise, and taking plenty of time to think about how it relates to you. Each title condenses that tool into a statement which you can repeat over and over in your mind to help you remember its main idea.

The book has a personal tone that speaks directly to those of you who are in recovery, but loved-ones and professionals will also gain insight and understanding. Although it is written in the first-person by Lindsey Hall, the thoughts and words come equally from Leigh Cohn.

Both of us welcome your feedback, and we invite you to contact us in care of Gürze Books, P.O. Box 2238, Carlsbad, CA 92008.

We are all worthy, but our problems prevent us from knowing this. The most important part of recovery is recognizing and enhancing our inherent worth. When we practice self-esteem, magical things happen. We love others. We attract good things to us. We "do the right thing" and if a decision does not turn out so well, we forgive ourselves. We experience feelings of all kinds. We are courageous, flexible, compassionate, humble, and funny.

Self-esteem is the purpose of my life. It sustains me emotionally, physically, and spiritually. It led to my own recovery from bulimia and to the discovery that I am a wealth of creativity and love. Just thinking about what my life is like now fills me with love. I am spilling over! I think about my parents with love, my siblings with love, old and new friends, my children, my work, the dog! When you practice self-esteem, you have an inner connection with everyone.

When I told people I was writing a book on self-esteem they looked at me with awe and said, "Oooooo!" and sighed deeply like I possessed some cherished gift. *It is a gift you can give to yourself.* These tools will help you do just that.

TOOL 1:

What's Your Problem?!

There are as many problems as there are people, more in fact. Maybe you think your problem is that you are an:

alcoholic,

bulimic,

drug abuser,

codependent,

victim of abuse,

child of a dysfunctional family,

shopaholic,

sex addict,

compulsive worker,

worrier,

generally unhappy person,

or any combination of these and other negative thoughts and behaviors. You may even define yourself solely in these terms.

The fact of the matter is, though, that you are not your problem, and realizing this will separate it from you. Your problem isn't who you are, it's what you have used to protect your physical and emotional well-being. It's veiling who you are: an innately worthwhile source of awareness, knowledge, creativity, love, and joy. If you practice self-esteem based on the faith that this is who you really are, then your problem will dissolve.

Your problem is uniquely yours. It can be life-threatening (drug addiction or anorexia nervosa), life-damaging (codependency or compulsive gambling), or even socially acceptable (compulsive exercise or an addiction to perfection). It can be difficult to pin-point, like a tendency to worry all the time or create chaos in your life. Whatever the particulars of your problem, it is the result of your unique heredity and life experiences, including your beliefs, values, thinking patterns, fears, loves, etc. You are the one who lives with it day in and day out.

When is a problem a problem? How can you tell when something really needs to be changed? My definition of a problem is a lot like John Bradshaw's definition of compulsive-addictive behavior, which he describes in his book, *Bradshaw on the Family**, as "any pathological relationship with any mood-altering experience that has life-damaging consequences." I will use this definition when I refer to your problem, as well. If you consistently depend on a particular experience to feel good or avoid feeling bad, and your growth and happiness is hindered as a result, then you have a problem.

It probably didn't start out as a problem. Chances are

it felt like it was the solution to other problems. That was true in my case. When I was a teenager I had fat thighs, which now seems like a fairly innocuous concern, but at the time were a major source of embarrassment. I placed a high value on looking the way everyone else wanted to look—slim—and thought that people who were thin had better lives. When I failed at conventional dieting, throwing up seemed like a good way to lose weight. It took care of fat thighs and an apparent lack of willpower, because I could eat whatever I wanted and be thin, too.

After a while, though, I wanted to binge and purge all the time. I had developed bulimia and it was taking care of more than just my fear of fat. It was my security blanket, companion, decision-maker and hiding place. From it I got a physical high, feelings of intimacy and sexuality, and a predictable way to cope with what seemed like an unpredictable world. The best thing I got was numbness. I could be in the world, but not of it. When I felt separate and afraid, and I needed a way to feel bonded with something—*anything,* I bonded with my bulimia. This seemingly innocent solution to weight control became a "pathological relationship with life-damaging consequences."

The time came, though, when my solution didn't work as well as it once had. This is true of most of our habitual coping mechanisms. What relieved our stress and tension, now adds to it. What gave us feelings of safety and well-being, now increases our guilt and shame. We want to hide. We may develop physical symptoms, stop taking care of ourselves, and give up hope. What gave us a feeling of being in control is now controlling us. Our moods swing between elated and angry, sad, ashamed and back to elated again. What used to solve problems becomes one in itself, while the original ones still remain. We layer problems on top of problems.

The challenge of recovery is to understand our problems and *do* something about them. Practicing self-esteem is one of the most effective catalysts for this, because when we can feel our own goodness, we are willing to do whatever it takes to love rather than harm ourselves. In this way, self-esteem is the means to recovery *and* it is the goal. In the moment and in the long run, it leads to happiness, peace, and the discovery of an innately worthwhile source of love that dwells within each of us.

If you've relied on specific feelings and behaviors for years and years, you may not believe that there could be something else to carry you over life's obstacles. There is something. It's the power of knowing who you really are, loving who you really are, and seeing that same essence in others and loving them. The way to quit living your problems is to practice a state of love and self-esteem. The tools and exercises in this book are designed to help you do just that.

Exercise:

What's Your Problem?

Throughout this book, "your problem" is mentioned, and this exercise will help you define your problem more clearly. This is the first step in separating it from you. Later, you might give different answers to these same questions. That's okay. This will give you a starting point.

I suggest writing your answers, because it is easier to be honest on paper than in the mind. Writing also allows you to see progress. Remember, this is your recovery and these are your words. You can scribble them or write them on a word processor. If writing is too much, dictate them into a tape recorder. Just let the words flow!

1. In a few words, what's your problem?

2. What makes it a problem?

3. How long has it been a problem?

4. What happened to you about the time it started?

5. How much time do you spend on it?

6. Does anyone else know about it?

7. How does it feel in your body, mind, and heart?

TOOL 2:

Your problem has served you well.

I n the past few years, there has been a recovery renaissance. We've got national organizations and local chapters devoted to recovery, seminars, workshops, support groups, treatment facilities, addictionologists, help-lines, newsletters, radio shows, television specials, news features, educational programs, fund raisers, home videos, audio tapes, and books such as this one for problems of all kinds! The fact that this enormous network exists and is flourishing is testimony to our myriad of problems and low self-esteem.

Many new ideas have been put forward which have revolutionized our thinking about the causes, consequences, and treatment of these problems. A vast number of people who have committed their lives to recovery are digging down deep in their souls to understand what happened to them and why. What they are finding is that *whatever they considered to be their problem was serving to protect them from painful feelings.*

There are many different kinds of painful feelings. Fear is a biggie. We're afraid of being abandoned or rejected. We're afraid to be alone. We're afraid someone might hurt us or not like us. We're afraid that this may be all there is to life. We rage. We feel helpless because we are treated unfairly and can't or don't protest. We don't feel loved enough and don't know how to ask for more. We are confused because what people say and what they do are often two different things. Most devastating of all is the feeling that we have no worth.

Where do feelings of worthlessness come from? Many come from our families, since more than 80% of our waking hours up to the age of eighteen are spent under their direct influence. During our most impressionable early years, the percentage is even higher. This is when we separate from mother's body to discover who we are. We search for identities in the mirroring eyes of our families. What if they don't have self-esteem? How can they teach it to us? If they treat us in ways that indicate to us that we are insignificant, incompetent, or unworthy, we believe them. This hurts.

We are also influenced by our society, culture, peers, heredity, and other factors. Many of the messages we get about ourselves from these sources are confusing, and make us feel inadequate as well. For example, when society places a high value on thinness and we have genetically chunky thighs, we feel ugly. When we see happy television families solve their problems in thirty minutes, and our family is a mess, we think there's something wrong with us. What chance is there for high self-esteem if our churches tell us we are born sinners?

What do we do about this pain? We adapt. We do whatever is necessary to secure emotional and physical survival. Often this means denying, repressing, and dissociating from the self we have come to believe is so bad. We present an adapted identity which is designed uniquely for our situation, and resort to all kinds of behaviors, even destructive ones, in order to feel secure, cared for, approved of, and loved. Some of us never feel these ways, no matter what we do. The best we can hope for is to find something to numb our pain, and we become attached to that substitute because it serves us.

Janet Jacobsen's problem was an obsession with suicidal thoughts. When she was a child, her mother did not express emotions, and her older brother resented and abused her. Her dad actually pushed her away when she said "I love you" to him one Father's Day. In *Recoveries**, our anthology of true stories, she writes, "I can imagine my baby self observing, 'It's not safe to feel or to express. I get rejected, hurt, and sent away.' I was proclaimed 'ugly' and 'bad' by a mother who preferred that there be pleasantness at all costs. 'What's wrong with you?' she would ask."

Janet tried changing herself to get love and approval. In her teens she worked on her appearance to make herself noticeable, but that earned her a "bad" reputation rather than love. Later, she reversed her image, dressing conservatively and becoming an award winning "A" student.

Eventually the pain of not being loved no matter what she did was too much for Janet to bear. "I was caught on this pendulum for years, swinging between fear and anger, being a good girl and a bad girl, a wimp and a witch, until eventually, years later, this escalated to the extremes of a zombie-like deadness which could only be relieved by adrenalized acts of self-destruction. . . . Self-hate ate away at me like acid, until the only solution to end the suffering was death."

Janet's obsessive thinking of death compelled her to experiment with a series of mini-stabs at suicide. She slashed her wrists with a razor blade, overdosed on pills, and spent 36 hours in a coma after taking a lethal combination of alcohol and sleeping pills. Even though she did make actual attempts to die, her constant thoughts about suicide were her primary protection from the painful feelings of her life. *Thinking about dying helped Janet to live.* Her suicide plans allowed her to imagine what it would be like to be at peace, and it gave her a way to avenge the unhappiness she felt was caused by her mother. It was an ideal outlet for her negativity. This problem served her well.

Her most desperate solution was supposed to be her last. She planned to overdose on more than one hundred assorted pills, and then bury herself under a pile of rubbish where she would not be found. She writes, "I imagined that rats would be crawling around my body, gnawing on it. Dying beneath a pile of rubbish would be a statement of how I felt about myself and my life."

Janet had spent a lifetime without being committed to life or death, but faced with the finality of this act, she had a startling realization: "I could feel how attached I was to the thought of suicide. I realized that I was addicted to it and would reach for it like an alcoholic reaches for a drink.

It offered me an escape when pressures got too great, or when reality became too unpleasant. It gave me some feeling of control over my life. It had become a part of my identity and my sense of importance. As I'd once gathered evidence for why I should die, I now began to gather evidence for why I should live."

She devoted herself to the practice of self-esteem, using such techniques as meditation, changing her diet, exercising regularly, saying affirmations, visualizing change, peer-counseling, taking classes, hypnosis, Intuitive Massage, improving relationships, and prayer. She stopped being angry at her mother when she became aware that resentment only caused her more pain. After all of those years, Janet Jacobsen learned how to love herself.

It may be difficult to see what possible good could have come from your painful, lost years, or that you needn't be ashamed. The fact of the matter is, though, that your addictions, destructive behavior, and negative thoughts had value for you, which is why you used them. In a way, your problem has given you the time you needed to get ready. Before, you weren't ready to face the pain of your life, but now you are.

Now, it can serve you in another way. It can point you in the direction you need to go to rebuild your life. A full understanding of how your problem has served you will show you what you need to do to recover. You might not have a full understanding right away, but each new realization will strip away another layer of conditioning and make clear a next step.

Furthermore, you may be better off in the long run because you had that problem. Without it you would not be learning to love yourself or to handle painful feelings in healthy, life-affirming ways. You can survive <u>and</u> thrive.

Your problem served you well—it is not your enemy. You need to treat that problem with love and compassion because it really was the best way you knew how to cope. It has been your friend for a long time. Now it's time to make new friends.

Exercise:

How has your problem served you?

The point of this exercise is to see that your problem protected you from painful feelings. Write down as many things as you can think of, and return to your worksheet to add more thoughts as they come to you later.

1. Make a list of the ways your problem has served you.

2. What painful feelings has it replaced?

For example:

How it served	Painful feeling
relaxation	*anxiety*
companionship	*rejection*
entertainment	*boredom*
courage	*fear*

TOOL 3:

It takes courage to heal.

Recovery is scary. It's normal to be afraid, considering the task. You have to face the past and acknowledge the truth of how others have treated you or you have treated yourself. There may be things you don't know or like about yourself. You might have physical pain, sleepless nights, and tormented days during this period of change. If you are giving up an addiction, habit, or negative coping mechanism, you are likely to fear the unknowns of who you are and what life will be like without it. What if you fail? What if you succeed?

Being courageous doesn't mean being fearless. It means accepting that recovery is scary, allowing the fears to exist, and doing what needs to be done anyway.

One powerful illustration of this point is the story of Pat Snyder's recovery. She is a woman who went through years of therapy to understand and overcome a 22-year struggle with eating disorders. After six years of commitment and steady progress, she left therapy feeling good about herself and her life. She was accomplished, contributing, a happy wife and mother, and "felt 97-98% free" in her life. She even directed a non-profit eating disorders association and helped others in recovery. What she didn't know was that she had yet to touch on the major contributing factor to her eating disorder—she had been sexually abused as a child.

The tip-off came when she began having vague feelings of anxiety somehow related to her sexuality, and noticed she was eating more for no apparent reason. Faced with erratic eating behavior again and confusion about the anxiety, she trusted that her feelings held meaning, and re-entered therapy, where anger and the word "denial" kept coming up. Although she did not understanding the meaning or increasing intensity of her feelings, she continued to trust them.

Soon afterwards, a nightmare led her to suspect that she had been sexually molested as a child, though she had no idea where, when, or by whom. Subsequent nightmares hinted at the same horror. Despite her repulsion, she hoped her suspicions were true, because then her life-long struggle would finally make sense.

In an article she wrote for her association's newsletter, Pat explained why she wanted to find out what really happened to her, even if it meant going through Hell to find out. "I will allow no more barriers to keep me from the truth of my experience. There will be no more secrets; no more closed doors. All that was hidden will be revealed so that my healing can take place." Pat decided to be more courageous by checking into a five-day residential program for Adult Children of Dysfunctional Families. Still, the memories refused to come. Was it only in her mind?

It wasn't until a month later, while she was having a body massage, that she had her first actual memory of what had happened. "Much to my horror <u>and</u> relief my suspicions were validated. It was my grandfather who sexually abused me. He was the only man in my life as a small child. I loved him so, trusted him, and loved spending time with him. When I remembered him raping me, my feelings of anger, hurt, and betrayal were mixed with confusion and vulnerability. How could he have loved me and hurt me like that? I knew that there was much more to remember. Part of me wanted to, but another part was terrified."

Pat confronted as much as she could handle, even though each new step brought more horrifying recollections of abuse by other family members, as well. The truth of what had been done to her as a child was even worse than she had feared, but Pat pushed forward. She says, "The truth will set you free, but first it may make you miserable. If we continue to search for our truth within, and value our experience of life—what we have been through, who we are, and who we are becoming—then we can be free."

She realized that she was a survivor, and her eating disorder had been a valuable "survival technique." It was her way of handling the pain of her family's secret. She also realized that the enormous amount of energy she had spent maintaining the eating disorder could be better spent on recovery. *

Facing your fears with courage is a transforming experience, because acts of bravery connect you with your inner strength. Even a small act is a way of taking charge of your life and care of yourself. Saying "no" is an act of bravery for a compulsive people-pleaser. Going to a shelter for abused women is a huge statement of self-worth for a battered wife. It is courageous for someone with an eating disorder to look beyond food and weight to the emotional issues beneath the surface. Any action which proclaims, "I have a right to my feelings and the truth of my experiences. I have value, and I deserve goodness," is a big step for someone who has never before believed it.

Fear is not something we are, it's something we have. It passes. Pain passes, too. Keep your sights set on the rewards to be gained. Even though you might not know what those are now, people who have been in recovery know, and they can be good examples for you. They know the pain and fear, and they know that courage is something we all have inside of us. Tapping into our courage is an act of self-esteem. Be brave now, look for that source of power and courage that exists within you.

Exercises:

Encourage bravery!

Here are exercises to help you understand more about your fears, courage, and goals in recovery. I encourage you to use a notebook for the many written exercises that are provided in this book, and to actively do the exercises that require participation. Experience the tools instead of just reading them.

1. Write about three times in your life when you have been brave. What did you do? How did it feel?

2. List your fears about recovery.

3. Look people in the eye. Take the initiative to say, "Hello" to strangers. Most people are afraid to share even that much of themselves; they are afraid that others won't like them. Be brave!

4. Exclaim your bravery! Go to a mountain top, beach, woods, rooftop, or other empowering place. Clench your muscles and shout out, "I am somebody. I am worthwhile. I deserve to be happy. I can do anything it takes to _____ (fill in the blank). And I will!"

TOOL 4:

Our secrets keep us separate.

When we have a problem, we focus on it. It becomes alive, and we form an intense relationship with it. In the process, we sever the ties to our own selves and to other people. It is possible to re-establish these ties, however, by telling the truth. Honesty is an act of love, a way of valuing our relationships and ourselves.

When our minds are habitually altered, whether by drugs, food, lack of food, compulsive thoughts, or obsessive behavior, we think in distorted ways. We judge our problems unmercifully. We label them disgusting, weak, petty, self-centered, and hateful, and what's more, we see ourselves that way, too. We blame ourselves for having stooped so low. We see our problems as proof that we are bad people and filter out any information that tries to tell us differently. We think in extremes such as all bad or all good. We focus on the negative. We blow up small mistakes into giant reflections of disgrace. We come to think that our problem is most or all of who we are, having lost touch completely with our true nature.

We then assume that if other people knew our secrets, they would think we were horrible, just like we do. Since we are ashamed of ourselves, we think they would be ashamed of us, too. So, we lie and hide our problems. We present a false self and feel like nobody really knows us. Then we feel further shame because we have lied! It doesn't occur to us that all of those other people whose lives seem so perfect in comparison to ours may be struggling, too. It doesn't occur to us that it is our secrets which are keeping us separate. Nor does it occur to us that the way to connect with ourselves and others simultaneously is to tell the truth—just be honest.

It was that way for me. During my nine years of bulimia, I distanced myself from my family, did not confide in my friends, and had a superficial marriage with a man to whom I never showed my real self. The more time I spent bingeing and vomiting—and thinking about it— the more secrets I kept and compulsive rituals I practiced. I devised elaborate charades to hide myself from everyone.

As it happened, bulimia was a relatively unknown eating disorder at that time. In fact, the term "bulimia" did not even exist. I believed that I was the only person in the world who had such a bizarre and disgusting habit. I never told anyone about it. Neither my parents, husband, or former roommates knew. Then something happened which I interpreted as a miracle. I chanced upon one of the first magazine articles written about this disorder, and incredibly, the therapist who wrote the article lived minutes away from me. I took a leap of faith, contacted her, and thus began my recovery.

She was conducting support groups for women, and I joined one. At first I just listened and observed. Just the thought of sharing myself honestly with these strangers made me queasy! Having never been in therapy before, I did not know what to expect. What struck me right off was the way the members seemed to trust each other. I'd always kept my distance from people, especially women, and I wasn't sure how to act or what to say in this new situation. I knew, though, that this was my chance to start a new life, and so I told the truth of how awful my life felt and that my eating and vomiting was out of control. In the midst of strangers I began to feel less alone.

I also realized what strength there is in support groups and in the truth. When others shared with me, I wanted to comfort them and love them. When I shared myself, I felt love coming back to me, and it flowed from me to them and back. We were connected to each other by the bonds of a common problem, and treated each other as equals but with greater respect than we had been treating ourselves. We practiced being non-judgmental and accepting of each other, and I think this enabled us to feel more that way with ourselves. In this way, even though loving yourself is the ultimate goal, loving others can get you there, and the ultimate act of love is to tell the truth.

Shortly thereafter, I separated from my first husband, then met and fell in love with Leigh Cohn, my husband and the co-author of this book. Again, I had the opportunity to practice honesty, and I trusted him with the truth of my bulimia and recovery. He continued to encourage me to love myself because he did! He saw the same me that the members of my support group had revealed, a worthwhile, beautiful, loveable Lindsey, and gradually I began to see myself that way, as well.

As my self-esteem grew, my recovery from bulimia accelerated, and all of my relationships improved. Believe me, honesty, love, and compassion sure beat obsessing and feeling miserable.

You are not the only one who has problems! Think about these round numbers: ten percent of Americans are alcoholics, one of every three women has been sexually abused, 96% of us come from dysfunctional families of one kind or another, there are more than 22 million adult children of alcoholics, and virtually everyone is concerned about their weight! Many, many people have a gnawing emptiness inside that they try to fill with all kinds of diversions.

What all of these people are missing is a sense of self-esteem—a recognition of their own goodness. The place to get this is in a relationship with yourself and with others, based on honesty, acceptance, and unconditional love. Have you ever been to a support group? The people at those meetings are not there to judge each other, "Let's see, Agnes was a bad drunk, Murray was even worse." Everyone knows that the members also have problems, and support each other because of them. Try talking to professional counselors, your friends, family members, and anyone else who might help.

Get to know the people in your life, and let them know you. Share your recovery with them, and transform your relationships. The fact is that most people have gone through similar—though different—experiences. Accept them for who they really are, and learn from them. Give up the relationship with your problem. See the goodness within you that has been hidden and let others see it, too.

Exercise:

You are not the only one with problems.

Hiding your problem gives it importance, because you fear what others will think of you, but they have problems too. This exercise helps you realize this, and encourages you to be honest. The truth of your problem and the knowledge of theirs will bring you together.

1. List about ten people you know, including yourself.

2. Beside each name, give examples of what you think are or could be their problems.

3. Evaluate and label the problems with terms like: big, not such a big deal, so little it barely matters, etc.

4. How do they (or might they) handle their problems?

5. Write about the truth of your problem.

TOOL 5:

It's Your Recovery.

Some of the beliefs, values, and rules that we adopt throughout our lives cause us problems and conflicts because, although they may be right for others, they are wrong for us. This is also true of rules in recovery. Although it is worthwhile to find out what has worked for others, ultimately, you are the only one who can decide what is and is not appropriate for you.

In order to know what is best for us, it's helpful to examine our belief systems. From the time we are infants, we gather information and form conclusions which help us make sense of our families and our worlds. These belief systems give us feelings of security and guidance; eventually an identity. We believe what others believe, and value what they value in order to belong, to get approval and love. Our families probably have the strongest impact on us, but our culture and society also influence us through schools, workplace relationships, structured religions, media, advertiser-consumer roles, and peer groups. Practically everyone has opinions on how life should be lived and every situation is an opportunity to modify our belief systems.

On a daily basis, we don't really think about what our beliefs are because they often operate below the level of our conscious awareness. We may not even know why we think the way we do, because the roots are buried so deep in the past. It doesn't take much to embed a belief into our system. Whatever helps us get our needs met, whether we are children or adults, we will store as useful and try again. For example, if hiding feelings keeps peace in the family, then we believe that keeping feelings to ourselves is a good thing to do in our other relationships, as well. Even the belief that we are bad people can result from the need to make sense out of the way we are being treated.

The examples above illustrate one of the problems with beliefs, rules, and values that have their origins in the past and roots in our subconscious. Even though they might not apply in the present situation, they still affect it. Lessons learned long ago translate into shoulds, musts, and givens which dictate and limit how we think and behave today. We rarely question these lessons because they once helped us survive, emotionally or physically; but hiding feelings or believing we are bad people will not enhance our lives in the present.

Another problem with belief systems is inherent in the very way they are created. When we are unsure about what is the right behavior or choice in a particular situation, we usually look outside ourselves for external cues which might help us decide what to do. This applies to a choice as small as ordering the same meal as a dinner companion or as large as choosing a career or spouse to meet the approval of others. This is especially true for those who are accustomed to being punished for making mistakes. Their own spontaneous, creative selves are kept in check. This is co-dependency—living in response to others instead of ourselves.

Unfortunately, when we try to live up to someone else's standards, we feel incompetent and disconnected from our own selves. If we break their rules, we feel like a failure. If we follow their rules, we feel unfulfilled, because other people's standards come from *their* needs and experiences, not ours. Worst of all, we think we are bad people for not being able to succeed in a life where we didn't make up the rules.

The fact is that we are all separate, unique individuals whose experience and perception of that experience is different. What I perceive as the best thing for me to do in any given situation to secure my well-being is not necessarily what anyone else would perceive. My awareness is uniquely my own, and I am the only one who truly knows what is best for me.

Living your own life is scary. It means growing up, making your own choices. Some people might not like that you are making changes. They are used to having you just as you have been. Keep in mind, though, that they are not inside your head or your heart. Their experience of living is based on their own unique past and inherited or forged beliefs. Your experience and reality are separate. You can watch, listen, and imitate just as you always have, but ultimately you are left alone with your awareness and the moment at hand.

Saying "no" to someone else's beliefs does not mean you don't care for the person or appreciate their feelings, it's simply a way of caring for yourself and appreciating your own feelings. What you are saying is, in effect, "I value my opinion, and it's worth valuing. I'm capable of making choices. I have freedom to change my beliefs, behavior, and how I feel about myself. I can meet my needs in a healthy way. I'm creative. I can determine what's best for me."

By choosing our own standards, we set ourselves up to feel good by being in a relationship with our own selves. Remember, this is the the most direct route to self-esteem, because we are connected to our own abilities and goodness. We might feel proud for having taken initiative. If we follow our own rules, we get rewarded with feelings of accomplishment. If we break our own rules, we know that it is the rule that needs to be re-evaluated, not ourselves, and we are rewarded by the learning process.

Recovery is an opportunity to challenge existing beliefs and values to form a new philosophy of life. While it is true that your past may have been shared with others, your recovery is just for you. It is for this reason that although you can gain insight from others, you have to direct your own recovery. You are adjusting your belief system, becoming open to new values and rules that will benefit you in the present. Try any and every approach to recovery until you find out what works, and then stick with it as long as it continues to help you.

Recovery is like New Year's Eve at the stroke of midnight. It's a time to let go of beliefs that no longer serve you and value the ones that do. Embrace your new life with optimism and joy. Getting to know your belief system is another step in getting to know your own inner self. Challenging those beliefs which do not promote your health and well-being is practicing self-esteem.

Exercise:

Examine your "shoulds."

Although the example below is brief, you will want to write more extensive answers. Make lists, elaborate, get into it!

1. List rules and "shoulds" that you think no longer work for you.
   Example: I should not express anger.

2. Where did these ideas come from? List.
   The values of my family, my shyness, a bad experience with my fourth grade teacher, etc.

3. How did these ideas serve you in the past?

It sheltered me from frightening arguments.

4. Why don't they apply anymore?
   I think anger is healthy in some situations. Anger is a reality for me.

5. Are there new beliefs that may take their place?
   It's okay to express anger.

TOOL 6:

Recovery begins when you're ready.

Does this sound familiar? One day, you make a resolution to change. You feel good about yourself because of your decision. After a day or two of "white-knuckled" abstinence, you feel even better, but recovery is tougher than you expected. The voice in your mind whispers, "You've been good, just one time won't hurt." You give in and feel a confusing mixture of relief and shame. Although your mind tells you that it doesn't matter, your heart knows the truth. You have made this type of resolution before and it has never stuck.

Instead of getting down on yourself over failures to stick to your resolve, try accepting that you were just not ready for recovery. Maybe promising to quit tomorrow is part of your problem! I spent nine years with bulimia promising that "this" binge would be my last. I tore up old lists that said I would quit "today," and made new lists; but, the promises of hope, a better life, and feelings of renewal were just more bulimia rituals. In those days, I always gave in to the pressure to eat, promised myself again that this would be my last binge, and denied that I had a problem!

It is easier to be in denial! It is the first line of defense against the realities of a problem and the uncertainties of recovery. What we don't realize is that denial, like promising to quit tomorrow, is part of the problem. It allows us freedom to make poor choices and suffer the consequences without attaching much importance to either. It keeps us at a safe distance from the truths behind our problems. If we deny that drinking, yo-yo dieting, overworking, or feeling afraid is a problem, we can ignore the reasons why we do these things. The most insidious thing about denial is that by obscuring the truth, it keeps us from our inner selves, the source of self-esteem.

Denial, like any habit, has a life of its own. Not only does it perpetuate itself and your problem, it may also be supported by some of those around you. They want to believe that you don't have a problem, because it hurts them to see you hurting. People who are codependent may also have a vested interest in your not changing. If they have become dependent upon your staying sick and you get better, it means that they too must undergo some changes of their own. Who wants the pain? It may be easier for them to deny that you have a problem, too.

Breaking through denial is not easy. Admitting to a problem may seem like admitting failure. We were weak to need a coping mechanism to begin with and we were weaker to have gotten hooked. To ask for help because we cannot get unhooked by ourselves is further proof of how bad we are. What if we try and can't do it? What if we quit and our lives still feel crummy? What experience could possibly make us want to recover so much that we will commit to a completely new and different life?

Charlie McMordie denied his problem until he had reached the end of the line, and then he pushed one step further. His autobiographical chapter in *Recoveries** describes his cocaine addiction and recovery.

He writes about a weekend when he tried shooting up an entire ounce of cocaine. He said that he wanted to keep injecting more and more until he could no longer take it. He reasoned, "If I died it would be over, and I'd be free." At one point during that cocaine binge, he collapsed, had a seizure, and woke up later in another room. Then, "I pulled myself up and instinctively went back into the bathroom again. After nearly dying, I was standing there fixing another shot. I saw a sick person in the mirror, and I knew then that I had to change or die. The only answer seemed to be to leave the syringe alone, but not until I had finished the ounce."

If you think that was Charlie's turning point, you're wrong. He went on to destroy a marriage and spend a family fortune on cocaine and other drugs. Paranoia from long-term usage drove him to another precipice. He asked to borrow his father's gun because he thought that suicide was his only remaining option. His parents wisely took him to a hospital for treatment. Still, that was not Charlie's ultimate turning point. After five weeks of detoxification and in-patient treatment, he was sober, but he still did not appreciate how bad his life had become. His doctors convinced him to move to another facility in a distant state. This is what happened next:

"I resisted once again and thought these exact words, 'It'll be a cold day in Hell when I don't drink and get loaded.' Spiritual experiences are hard to explain, but I believe that God sent me a message that day. The plane landed for a stopover in Denver, and there were two feet of snow on the ground. It may not have meant anything to the other passengers, but that snow changed my life. I saw it as God's answer that it was a cold day in Hell, today! I finally admitted to myself that I was a sick junkie who could find a greater power to help me."

Charlie sums up his present outlook in this way: "Being clean and sober is first and foremost in my life, and only by being that way can I feel a part of a grand scheme. There's no growth or meaning when you have a tube in your nose or a needle in your arm. Trying to help others (as a counselor for chemically-dependent individuals) is important to me, and that just doesn't happen while using drugs. Now I have meaning in my life and it's better than it ever was before."

In Charlie's case, he saw a seemingly insignificant blanket of snow and it completely transformed his view of himself and his life. He had what Earnie Larsen calls "the conversion experience." In his book, *Stage II Recovery**, Larsen writes, "The conversion experience occurs when you hit rock bottom. It is then that you might have a spiritual experience that thrusts the decision to change upon you."

This, in my mind, is the experience which tells you that you are ready. Like Earnie Larsen, I label it spiritual, not in the religious sense, but in the sense of it touching your spirit. It is one where a connection is made between you and another person, place, or event that feels like a truth. Time stands still. It's as though you are receiving some kind of mystical hint that the universe cares about you and that you are deserving of such special attention.

This kind of experience is not the same for all people. You don't have to be on the brink of suicide or on the verge of an overdose. It might occur when a boss says "You're fired," when you see tears in your child's eyes, when a friend says they're worried about you, or simply when you catch your reflection in the mirror. It might be in the loneliness of boredom or the anxiety of a crowd. The only thing that is the same for everyone is the connection between themselves and the truth which breaks through their denial.

Furthermore, a conversion experience has meaning unique to the individual and is often the launching pad for a genuine decision to change. It makes clear that it is more painful to keep the problem than to let it go. Feeling bad about your failures will not help you reach this point. Actually, feeling bad about your failures is part of your problem and is only helping to keep it alive.

Be on the lookout for a conversion experience. It may have already happened, or perhaps it is in the reading of this tool! It might be miraculous or mundane, but it will speak directly to you. Even if it doesn't make clear the whole path of your recovery, it will encourage you to take one step; and, each subsequent step you take will be another affirmation of your strength and goodness.

Exercise:

What makes you think you're ready for recovery?

Think this question through and answer it honestly: What makes you think you're ready for recovery?

Examine other times you've decided to change and why this time is different.

TOOL 7:

Recovery is an on-going process.

I used to think that if I went for one day without overeating and throwing up, I would be recovered. I thought that my bulimic behavior was the only problem, and that not doing the behavior was the solution; but, when I stopped stuffing food down, up came feelings and questions about relationships, self-esteem, confidence, and beliefs. In the process of my recovery, all of those questions needed to be addressed. I realized that I had much more to recover from than just a food obsession.

What you think is your problem may actually be just the tip of the iceberg. Beneath the surface of your daily routine is a lifetime of experiences that got you there. Remember, your problem is a solution for easing your pain. That pain may reach far into your past, originating long before your current troubles. You've layered new problems on top of old ones, and may not be aware of the old ones that still exist.

Just as your problem developed over time, recovery must also take time. This is a hard one to accept. You wish it was as easy as throwing away your cigarettes or never taking another drink, but that isn't so. Mere abstention or "white-knuckled sobriety" does not take into account that your problem is a symptom of underlying issues which gradually make themselves clear as you proceed. Quitting the behavior is only a start. It's not surprising that this process takes so long, because there is so much to do and undo.

For this reason, you have to redefine recovery continuously as you get better. You're a different person after just one small step forward, and small steps lead to more steps. In the Twelve Step tradition, that is called taking it "one day at a time." This is the process of recovery, and guess what—this is the process of life. Here are some things to keep in mind:

• *The recovery process must have a beginning, and to be overwhelmed at first is normal.* Aside from the physical side-effects of ending an addiction, such as cravings or withdrawal, it is also common to have an onrush of emotions. Your problem has helped you avoid painful feelings, and without it they will surface. You may also be faced with repressed memories or emotional highs and lows.

Do not diminish the intensity of this period. I highly recommend that you have professional medical and psychological support.

• *Setbacks naturally occur.* How do you want to think about them? Will they be proof that you can't make it, your secret shame; or, is it possible for you to see them as lessons? Breaking your resolve does not mean that you have failed in your recovery, because setbacks are part of the process. Furthermore, many recovering people have said that their most valuable moments of insight were as a result of setbacks. This is not meant to encourage you, nor to diminish your motivation by condoning repeated destructive behavior, but one or two setbacks do not return you to the starting point. They must be examined and used to step forward.

Here's how a fellow-recovered bulimic described her learning process in our book, *BULIMIA: A Guide to Recovery:* "I had to accept that each time I decided not to throw up was an experience that I could add to my repertoire of getting better. A failure did not mean all was lost. I could decide not to throw up next time. At those times I would make use of the failures by examining the circumstances. At first, I thought this was weak—that I 'should' be able to face anything to really be getting better. But I also had to face that I needed to build up my repertoire of holding in food so I could get stronger. I became more self-accepting which enabled me to feel better about myself. I began to carefully examine how I felt after I had thrown up and also how I felt when I didn't. I gained greater trust in myself and in my ability to get well if I chose to."*

• *Recovery will mean different things to you as you proceed.* It's not just about ending destructive behavior. One breakthrough will lead to another as you gradually become free of all limitations, conditioning, and whatever stands in the way of your self-discovery. There is no way to know what lessons will be easy and which will be hard. Your goals, values, self-image, abilities, and so on will change as this transformation occurs.

• *You may find that the recovery process does not have the end that you thought it would have.* You won't wake up one day and find yourself magically cured. You will probably find that your definition of "recovery" becomes less associated with your problem and more centered on self-esteem and the process of living.

I suggest being gentle at first. Give yourself time. Give yourself credit. Keep in mind that even a small success can bring big feelings of competence. Pat yourself on the back. Literally! It feels silly, but it gets the message across clearly. Take one step at a time in a positive direction; this is the practice of self-esteem.

Exercise:

Affirm your recovery process.

Complete these sentences with pats on the back:

1. Lately, I've been more willing to . . .

2. Something I see differently now is . . .

3. . . .had a powerful effect on me.

4. One of the ways I'm changing is . . .

5. It is getting easier for me . . .

6. I realize I can choose . . .

7. A year from now I . . .

8. I am grateful . . .

TOOL 8:

Whatever you do matters.

Sometimes our problems take on such grotesque proportions that we are immobilized. We feel ineffective, dwarfed by them, and we resist taking any steps to change the situation. The problems seem to take on lives of their own, making decisions for us. We give them the responsibility for our choices because we are afraid of failure, risk, challenge, change, repercussions, not being the best, unhappiness, insignificance, uncertainty, dreaming, love—LIFE. We give up experiencing our lives to the experience of our problems.

What's more, if we can't do anything about our problems, the thought that we have any impact on the rest of the world seems absurd. So, we live in isolation. We don't have time for anyone or anything other than our problems. They are what matters. We have no connections or meaning apart from them.

The fact is that you do not live in a vacuum. Everything you do matters. You have an impact on others, and so does your problem. One word, a look, the inflection in your voice, even your body odor affects someone! You don't even know who is affected by the deeds you do as you continue along your course and they along theirs. What's more, everything you think and do has some kind of effect on you, as well.

Good begets more good, negative thoughts and actions produce negativity. Which do you prefer? Think of your self-esteem like an infectious flu virus. You have the flu and give it to your coworkers, friends, family, and others. Your grocer catches the flu from you and gives it to a news reporter who gives it to a camera operator who is there to interview the President of the United States. He catches that same virus and gives it to other world leaders at the United Nations, who in turn spread it throughout the world. You made a tremendous global impact just by sneezing!

Substitute the flu virus with how you live your life. If you are honest, loving, nurturing, and positive with yourself, that rubs off on others. The line from Michael Jackson's song, *Man in the Mirror*, sums it up well, "If you want to make the world a better place, take a look at yourself and make a change."*

Let me tell you about Robert Sundance. He was one of the chapter authors from our book *Recoveries*—a hopeless drunk! I can't think of anyone who had a worse existence and accomplished so much. He began drinking at age three, and spent more than twenty years drunk and homeless on skid row. You've seen the kind of guy. He slept in parking lots, bought cheap wine with any money he could scrape together, and was in the drunk tank more than 500 times. He wrote, "I'd wake up so damn sick, I'd have to drink at least a quart of wine just to get straight enough to get up. Whiskey is too strong. Wine is the only thing that'll calm the nerves and make you feel better."

For decades, he had no contact with his family, and his only friendships were with other winos who drifted in and out of town in railroad box cars or drunk tanks. During one ten year period, he spent an average of 226 days per year in jail. He saw people die, tagged for the morgue with no name of their own, lives without meaning. It doesn't get much lower than that.

In jail, he took up a one-man cause against the illegality of public drunkenness, arguing that alcoholism was a disease. He believed that to lock people up for being alcoholic was like arresting people for being diabetic and that no one should be treated that way. He wrote letters, studied law books checked out from jail libraries, and filed petitions—eighty of them in ten years. Most importantly, he refused to plead "guilty" to public drunkenness. The courts, however, would not hear his case, held him over for trial, and then dismissed the case months later after his stay in jail exceeded the punishment for being guilty. For fifteen years in Los Angeles, he was caught in that cycle until an ambitious lawyer from a public agency became interested in his case, bailed Sundance out of jail—the first time that had happened in 30 years—and arranged for him to enter a treatment program.

Sundance's recovery was understandably difficult. At that point, his goal was to have his day in court, not to quit drinking. He skipped out of the facility to have a drink, got kicked out of treatment, and ended up back in jail twelve more times before his lawyer convinced him that he had to be sober to be effective. He finally entered a program wanting to stick to it. Driven by a single-minded goal, he dedicated his efforts to getting sober, and with the help of treatment professionals and public assistance, he stopped drinking.

Sundance became an outspoken critic of the legal system and an advocate of sobriety. He eventually won his case, and as a result, public drunkenness arrests in Los Angeles County dropped from more than 50,000 to about 1,000 a few years later. Within ten years of his legal victory, 35 states decriminalized public drunkenness.*

We can't all be revolutionaries; most of us wouldn't want to be. It's hard enough doing good things for ourselves, much less the world; but even small acts of caring matter, as do callousness or ambivalence. By choosing to make that one small positive change, you are affirming, "What I do matters," which in effect says that what we all do matters. "I have worth; we all have worth. I deserve love and compassion; we all do. My life has value; our lives have value. Life is valuable!" In their own way, these are revolutionary thoughts. Their essence is that all of us have worth, though we may not know it. The results of this approach to people and to life are far reaching.

Life's steps go from moment to moment in a straight line, but the people and events around you are gently swayed, by your every move like the ripples in a pond. Improve the world by valuing your self! It matters! Prove that your life has meaning and value—it does.

Exercise:

Think one thought of love all day.

Here's a challenge. Pick one thought of love. Write it down on a slip of paper and carry it around in your pocket. Repeat it to yourself often throughout the day. See what happens.

Having trouble knowing where to start? Try some of these:

- Everyone is a unique and worthwhile person.
- Wherever I am, love is.
- I will only speak positively.
- Every day in every way is getting better and better.
- I will treat myself and everyone I meet with love and respect.
- Life is a treasure.

TOOL 9:

Who are you?

In this tool, I'm going to ask you to celebrate your strengths and devalue your weaknesses. Although you may be tempted to skip by this one because it might be painful to honestly admit to faults, it is meant to show you how few faults you really have.

I once heard a therapist say, "The hardest thing for people with low self-esteem to do is to accurately describe themselves." Here are some reasons why it might be difficult:

1. You dwell on your problems and ignore your good points.
2. You feel more comfortable with faults.
3. You look outward for self-definition.
4. It is painful.
5. You are ashamed.
6. There are some things you don't know about yourself.

Let's examine these reasons more carefully:

1. You dwell on your faults and ignore your good points.

When you think of yourself, you mostly see your faults as though they make up the whole or the most important parts of you. If you have a problem, you may even experience it—with all its compulsion, frustration, weakness, and negativity—as who you are. In my case, for example, instead of seeing myself as a worthwhile, multifaceted individual who happened to use binge-eating as a coping mechanism, I thought of myself as bulimic, and therefore worthless.

2. You feel more comfortable with faults.

Sometimes it is more comfortable to think poorly of yourself. If it is a habit reinforced by others or yourself, it has support in your life. Being down on yourself is a way of giving up the responsibility for making scary changes. It is a way of esteeming others, of pleasing them and taking care of their needs. That role may be comfortable for you. Further, being down on yourself can give you attention, security, control, and may seem like a "normal" approach to life.

3. You look outward for self-definition.

This is the land of the "shoulds." Instead of looking inward at yourself to realize, "I am. . ." you look outward and think, "I should be." You think you should be thinner, richer, happier, more in control, better liked, or different than you are. You're living in the future instead of the now. This creates both pressure and shame.

You think you don't measure up, and worse yet, you think other people know you don't measure up. It's all mind-reading anyway. You're worrying about what you think others are thinking about you! It's bases loaded in the World Series, the manager, pitcher, catcher, and shortstop huddle on the pitcher's mound, and you think they're talking about you!

4. It is painful.

When you use a facade to cover over painful feelings, it hurts to uncover the pain. It is easier to present a false front and deny or repress the "real" you who hurts. You don't want to know the truth.

5. You're ashamed.

You're ashamed of having your problem, because it proves you're weak, worthless, and different. Of course, you don't want to accurately describe yourself because then you would see how self-destructive you really are. If you don't tell the truth, then you can just go on, avoiding the issue. You're also ashamed of this deception.

6. There are some things you don't know about yourself.

If you have been in a rut, you are blind to some of your qualities. These could be strengths or weaknesses, but a rut is a rut. You can't see sunlight if you have your eyes closed. You can't see yourself if you don't look. That is why this tool encourages you to look at who you really are.

Exercise:

Take a personal inventory.

The purpose of this exercise is to describe yourself, celebrate your strengths, and change your perception of the negatives. Write out your answers. Emphasize your positives and restate your negatives.

1. Celebrate your strengths. These are things you like about yourself or your life. Here are a few ways to celebrate your strengths:

- With affirmations
  I'm a good friend! People like my sense of humor, I love to make them laugh, and they can count on me because I'm reliable. I listen and sympathize. No wonder they like me!

- Use superlatives
  My wonderful home is a fantastic place!

- Imagine how your best friend would positively describe you.

2. Devalue your negatives. These are things you don't like about yourself or your life. Here are a few ways to devalue your negatives:

- Restate them using accurate, nonjudgmental language.
  Restate, "I'm too fat!" to "I weigh 190 pounds." or "I smoke too much." to "I use cigarettes to relieve my stress."

- See that many negatives have corresponding positives.
  "I cry too easily." to "I am a sensitive person." or "I am a workaholic." to "I have a tremendous amount of creative energy."

- Practice acceptance of those negatives which you are unwilling or unable to change at this time.
  "I'm ashamed of being a drug addict." to "I accept that I choose to use drugs instead of going through the pain of recovery." or "I'm afraid of intimacy because I was raped." to "I accept that I was raped, and it may take me a while to be capable of intimacy."

- Imagine how your best friend would describe your negatives. Remember, they like you regardless of your faults.

▼

TOOL 10:

Know where you are going and how to get there.

Have you given much thought to why you are alive, whether your life has meaning, if you are on Earth for a reason? What do you want out of life? Do you want to be a happy person, successful, be in love, feel safe, or make a difference to the world? Do you know how to achieve this? Do you know when an immediate decision will help you reach your goals or move you further from them?

People addicted to their problems are cut off from their long-term goals. They usually have a hard time answering the question, "What do you want out of life?" They are unaware of or give little value to their own dreams. They also allow their problems to dictate for them what they will do in the short term. When confronted with the choice between feeling pleasure (or the absence of pain) or moving towards recovery, they choose temporary, immediate, gratification. They get "high" or escape into the moment, and when the moment passes, they have feelings of guilt, failure, and worthlessness.

People in recovery are willing to at least try to make decisions about what they want. A life beyond addiction is important to them. They force themselves to think about long-term goals even though the future is abstract, and focusing on their own wants is uncomfortable and unfamiliar.

Even with recovery as the top priority, small daily decisions are often agonizingly difficult. Should I eat the cheesecake? If I call my mother, will I feel better or worse? Can I afford therapy? Faced with these questions, temptations and daily pressures, individuals in recovery are learning to give up feelings of stopgap pleasure, banking on feeling good about themselves in the long run. For a compulsive eater, saying, "No, I won't eat the cheesecake," is an empowering step which connects them to their goal. "Recovery" is a concept, decisions are goals in action.

When in doubt about a decision, ask yourself the following question: Which choice will further my ability to love myself? Even long-term wants can be clarified by this question. Are you wondering how you would know what will further your ability to love yourself?

Each of us has an *inner voice* that has our best interests at heart. It's the one that is urging us to recover, saying, "You are worth it." Sometimes it is faint, sometimes thunderous. There are other voices that argue with it, saying, "One drink won't hurt. I'm weak. Do it later." It's a lot like the cartoons with the good angel and bad devil trying to persuade the innocent mouse. Listen to the good one! It's really that simple of a premise, or as Dean Acheson, former Secretary of State has often been quoted, "When in doubt, do the right thing."

Further, how we respond to this inner voice determines how we feel. When we don't listen to the inner voice—or can't listen because our problems are the only things we hear—we feel bad. When we follow its lead with the faith that it is guiding us towards what's best for us, we feel good. We have taken a step towards something we want. We are valuing our own needs. We are developing and nurturing a relationship with our own selves and therefore are practicing self-esteem. This relationship, this friendship with ourselves, will ultimately help us achieve our immediate, short-term, as well as long-term, goals.

Throughout time people have pondered their existence, searching for the meaning of life. Philosophers, theologians, politicians, bartenders, hair dressers, and everyone else has an opinion. It is an ageless question about which volumes have been written. Let me put in my two cents worth: LOVE YOURSELF. There is no greater purpose in life. Your inner voice tries to tell you this, but your problems are so loud you can't hear it!

Of course, you may think that your purpose in life is to feed the starving, provide for your family, do good work, glorify God, or just sleep; but, to fully do any of these things, you must love, honor, and respect your own self.

Then, you will know the true depth and breadth of your abilities and capabilities. You will be able to give more of yourself to the starving, your family, job, and God. You'll also sleep better!

Setting goals and reaching for them can be two effective ways to practice self-esteem, because both force you to spend time with yourself, valuing your experience. Self-esteem can thus be viewed as the means to recovery and the outcome, because it not only benefits your daily quality of life, but also furthers your goals. It is something you can practice until it becomes second nature. Hopefully, it will become your first nature!

It may feel selfish to give your own wants value. It may feel egotistical to practice loving yourself, or even futile to dream; but, no matter what you want to do, who you want to be, whatever your situation or purpose in life, self-esteem—a relationship with your own inner self—is the key.

I recently learned of the death of my childhood friend, John. He had AIDS. When I think back to our gang of friends during my early school days, John stands out as a reckless, attractive, fun-loving guy. Although we grew apart as we got older, I heard that he continued to live recklessly, using drugs and alcohol. In his late twenties, he acknowledged to himself and others that he was gay. He frequented bath houses and had anonymous sex with many men. When his parents rejected his lifestyle, he essentially told them to drop dead. He had no purpose or goals, and drifted from city to city and job to job without focus.

When he first tested positive for the HIV virus, he drank and used drugs to greater excess. He hoped death would come quickly and without pain, but developed no AIDS symptoms for over a year. When it appeared that he was not going to die soon, he began to change. He stopped loading his body with toxins and his life with negativity. He dedicated himself to more healthy living, and in the process came in touch with the inner self that he had kept hidden for so long. It was around this time that John called me. He was reestablishing contact with friends, had healed family wounds, and told me that he was trying to find himself.

I got a letter from him when he was hospitalized for pneumonia, about two months before he died. He wrote, "I'm almost thankful that I got AIDS. Without it, I might never have known who I am. For all of these years, I was detached from my own self, not even aware that there was another perspective on life. I probably would have continued on without having any meaningful relationships, but now I cherish the love of my family and friends. AIDS has helped me to see my reason for being alive—to love and be loved. Whatever happens in this life or beyond, I am at peace with myself."

It's never too late to discover the source of love that dwells within you, that has your best interest at heart. Listen to your inner voice and give it value. Allow it to guide you in your recovery.

Exercise:

Goal setting

Your answers to these questions reflect your feelings at this given time. You might answer differently tomorrow or next week. Since this is the case, I encourage you to write down your answers today, date them, and review them in the future. You might want to repeat this exercise over and over throughout your recovery and your life.

1. What is your purpose in life?

2. What are your long-term goals that will move you towards your greater purpose in life?

3. What are your short-term goals that will move you towards your long-term goals?

4. What immediate choices are you in the process of making?

5. How will practicing self-esteem help you achieve what you've answered above?

TOOL 11:

You have to add something if you are taking something away.

Who are you without your problem? If you quit today, what would be left of you? I can remember being so consumed by bulimia that I feared the emptiness of a life without it. If I wasn't bingeing, it was on my mind. I even dreamed about food. I spent so much time obsessing, it seemed unfathomable to me that I could fill my days without bingeing. What would be left if I took it away? What would I do instead?

When you take away your problem, something must be added to take its place. There is no other possibility. If you went to the same restaurant every day for all of your meals, and the restaurant burned down, would you stop eating? Would you stand in the rubble that was once a building and wait for your food? Of course not!

When you incinerate your addictions, obsessions, coping mechanisms, negative behaviors, and self-defeating attitudes you have to rely on something else. Find out what works for you by trial and error. Some of your choices may not help, others may work for a while and then won't anymore. See what feels right.

It's not unusual for people to give up one negative behavior and take on another. If you are used to negative coping, it's logical that you might follow the same pattern again. That's why some A.A. meetings are in smoke-filled rooms, with plenty of coffee available. This is not a criticism. The choices of nicotine and caffeine are positive steps for some recovering alcoholics. As their recoveries progress, they will probably give up on those compulsions as well. Face it, a lot of us have compulsive personalities. That's not bad or good. It is just the way we are. If we can't change how we are, we can at least try to be compulsive about moving in a positive direction.

Transformations of thoughts and behaviors take place gradually. Be gentle with yourself. You are not a failure at recovery because everything doesn't change overnight. Abstinence can be immediate, but damaged relationships do not instantly heal, nor do hurt feelings. Some things cannot be changed at all, like other people, situations, or the past. What you are faced with is changing your own immediate experience from feeling bad to feeling good by choosing to love yourself *as much as you can* from one moment to the next.

When you decide to make a change, you might find it helpful to say good-bye to what you are leaving behind. Perhaps you need to grieve for the problem you are casting away. Allow yourself to cry, feel angry, or be nostalgic about the past. It is appropriate to feel your loss. You will surely miss the old ways, but letting them go is the only way to make room for the new.

A ritual might make your good-bye more real or more effective. Many cultures have rites designed to purify and bring health, happiness, and peace to the participants. The Cherokee Indians immerse themselves in flowing water, like a stream, and release an object symbolizing their problem, allowing it and their attachment to it to float away. (A priest standing downstream retrieves the item and buries it.) Another ritual is the *Rudra Yajna*, a fire purification ceremony practiced in India. The smoke from this fire, which is made extremely pungent by the addition of aromatic herbs, spreads through the air, cleansing everyone and everything it touches. Sometimes participants mentally toss their impurities into this fire. Actually, these ceremonies are considerably more involved than I've described, but the essence of both is similar.

Why not try something like them? Water can have a wonderfully purifying affect. Doesn't everything seem a bit fresher after it rains? Create your own water rite. . . or fire ritual. Add incense, herbs, or eucalyptus leaves to a roaring fire. On slips of paper, write your problem and anything else you want to let go. Breathe in the power of the fire and toss in your papers! Perhaps you don't go in for such elaborate rituals. A bath, sauna, or watching the sunset may be enough. The importance does not lie in what you do so much as in the connection you are making with your desire and willingness to change. You are letting go of whatever stands in the way of your recovery and practice of self-esteem.

When you make the choice to let go of a significant part of your life, you are creating a space. You will find that you have time to fill, energy to expend, and emotions to handle. How you choose to fill the void is up to you. Whatever you do will be new and different, and you may not get as much immediate satisfaction or relief. For example, taking long walks, listening to music, or gardening is just not the same as abusing food, drugs, or alcohol; it's a different kind of "high." It is difficult to substitute forgiveness or acceptance for anger, confidence for helplessness, clarity for confusion, or loving yourself for despising yourself. Try not to get too discouraged; you're building a new life!

You may not know specifically what to do, but ultimately it does not matter. New activities provide a break from the old; they fill the void. Pick whatever you think may give you a rest from obsessing. You do not have to always be <u>working</u> at your recovery, sometimes <u>playing</u> is what you need. Self-inquiry is important, but so is zoning out in front of the television and resting your mind! The ultimate rewards are not going to come from specific activities, but from the time devoted to taking care of yourself.

Exercise:

These are a few of my favorite things.

What are you going to do instead of your problem? This exercise is intended to help you think of some positive choices. Chances are it will be hard for you to name many favorite things to do because you've been relying on your problem for so long. Experiment. Try to remember what you used to enjoy before you had your problem. What did you do for fun as a child?

1. Make a list of at least fifteen "B" activities that you enjoy (or have an inkling that you might enjoy). "B" activities are things you do for fun, as opposed to "A" activities, which are things that must be done (work, hygiene, buying groceries, going to the bank, etc.).

2. Do at least two "B" activities every day. If you don't have at least two each day, you're not trying *easy* enough!

Here are some items from my "B" activity list:

Gardening	*Soaking in a hot bath*
Swimming	*Walking the dogs*
Making soft-sculpture dolls	*Fixing things*
Being romantic with Leigh	*Sweeping out the garage*
Reading books to the kids	*Playing the piano*
Talking with friends & family	*Writing letters*
Doing yoga	*Meditating*

TOOL 12:

Don't be afraid of mistakes.

We think we shouldn't make *misteaks,* but everyone does! Actually, the mistake isn't in the making or doing of something "wrong," but rather in our attitude about it. People with high self-esteem know they're doing their best. They are willing to learn from mistakes and feel good about themselves in spite of them or while correcting them. People with low self-esteem feel awful about their mistakes and are immobilized by the fear that they will make more.

What are mistakes anyway? In truth, they are simply labels that we apply to our actions in retrospect. Mistakes do not occur at the moment of decision or action, because at that moment we are doing what we think serves us best. Later, we call something a mistake when we have experienced the consequences of it, and can see that we could have or should have acted or chosen differently. Certainly, some of these "mistakes" are legitimate goofs, like wrong turns and broken dishes. More often than not, though, our "mistakes" are simply the result of our limited awareness at the time.

Why, then, do we feel so badly about ourselves after we have made what we call a mistake? We walk around silently insulting ourselves with thoughts like, "I put my foot in my mouth again. I sure blew it that time. I'm so stupid! What's the matter with me?" Why is it so easy to think poorly of ourselves?

The reason is that we are conditioned to think that what we do is a reflection of who we are inside. We learned this as kids and believe it as adults! We have misconceived notions that: doing bad means being bad, and conversely, doing good means being good; doing well in school means we're good, doing poorly means we're bad; having a clean room means we're good, living in a pig sty means we're pigs; being thin means we are a better person than if we are fat. We think that all of the outer appearances of living, such as what we do, look like, choose for a mate, etc. reflect on our value as individuals.

Rarely do we acknowledge that we are all just doing our best. Some of us are unforgivingly critical of everyone: friends, relatives, employees, the government, our favorite sports teams, baggers in the grocery store, and subsequently, ourselves. We don't realize that every judgement, comparison, and criticism we make of someone else is felt at some level by us. When we devalue them, we unwittingly devalue ourselves. Sometimes, practicing compassion with other peoples' mistakes will produce compassion for our own. Stop judging and criticizing others! Can you hear yourself?

What we don't realize is that no matter what decisions or actions we perform, no matter what we look like, where we live, what we own, we remain worthy, important, lovable people. Our value as a human being is not based on our behavior no matter what label we put on it, mistake or success, hero or homeless. *We* are not *what we do.* It is important to separate the two. There is no blueprint for living. Our bodies did not come with an instruction manual, and our lives are not based on following specific directions to get perfect results. We are born infinitely loveable and loving souls doing our best to survive physically, emotionally, and spiritually.

Self-esteem is a relationship with your own self. Labeling something as a mistake and judging yourself as bad for having made it gets in the way of that relationship. Matthew McKay and Patrick Fanning elaborate on this idea in their excellent book *Self-Esteem,* "Self-esteem has nothing to do with avoiding mistakes. Self-esteem is rooted in your unconditional acceptance of yourself as an innately worthy being, regardless of mistakes. Feeling good about yourself is not something you do after all mistakes have been corrected—it's something you do in spite of mistakes."*

People with problems think they've made some enormous mistakes and feel rotten about themselves as a result. They make that connection between what they have done—like being hooked on substances, thoughts, or behaviors—and who they are. They label their actions and therefore themselves as "wrong, disgusting, a mistake, weak, foolish, etc." Obviously, these kinds of thoughts sabotage recovery! There is no strength or motivation behind self-criticism even if you think you deserve it. As Aldous Huxley wrote in *Brave New World,* "If you have behaved badly, repent, make what amends you can and address yourself to the task of behaving better next time. On no account, brood over your wrongdoing. Rolling in the muck is not the best way of getting clean."*

Choosing recovery is a courageous step. It means accepting that everyone makes mistakes, even you. It means forgiving yourself for the mistakes you've made. It means being willing to take risks in spite of the fact that you probably will make more mistakes along the way. If you are used to thinking that your life is one big mistake, believing yourself to be valuable in spite of it all is like being reborn. What's more, changing those perceptions is hard labor! It takes courage and persistence. Remember, your worth is a fact—whether or not you believe it and act on it is up to you!

Thinking about mistakes in a different way will raise your self-esteem. See them as opportunities to know yourself better, or blessings in disguise. They can be teachers or warnings. At the very least, they shed light on your choice and help you to see that you can choose differently next time. Someone in recovery who has a setback can label it as a mistake and feel that they and their recovery are failures, or they can examine why they made the choice that they did and grow from it. Perhaps that lesson will prevent future setbacks. In this way, their "mistake" served them well.

As you practice thinking about your mistakes in a more compassionate way, you raise your self-esteem. As you raise your self-esteem, being compassionate with yourself becomes easier. Once again, self-esteem is both the means to recovery and the goal. It does not prevent you from making mistakes, because you will always make some, but it keeps your mistakes from disrupting your progress.

Things are not always what they appear. Mistakes happen—sometimes for the best. Columbus was going to India!

Exercise:

Rethinking "mistakes"

Write your answers to the following:

1. Describe one specific mistake you recently made.

2. How did you feel about yourself?

3. What were the immediate consequences?
   What came later?

4. Why did you call it a mistake?

5. What did you learn from your mistake?

6. Fill in the blanks using your own words to affirm your self-esteem:

"Even though I _____ (your mistake), I am still _____ (a worthwhile person)."

TOOL 13:

Acceptance transcends control.

Our society places a high value on control. We think that it is a sign of strength, success, and good character. It is something we should strive for, an admirable quality. We are afraid of people who appear to be out of control like the mentally ill, junkies, prostitutes, people covered with tattoos, and other "fringe" people. We are even afraid to get close to friends and relatives who have problems like obesity, anorexia, alcoholism, or chronic lying, because they appear to be out of control—connected to something within themselves that we don't understand. We don't want to face that this same something exists within us; a dark side, a propensity for doing what is not in our own best interests, a need to escape.

This fear comes from our low self-esteem. We have blown our problems and negative self-image way out of proportion, and assume that if we weren't "in control," we would only make bad choices and chaos would reign in our lives. We think we *need* control because we don't trust our own goodness, and we don't trust our own goodness because we don't know ourselves very well. We operate under the assumption that we are bad, but it's just not true!

We have difficulty seeing our true nature, that this "dark side" of ours is only a small part of who we are. It exists, but so does our "bright side," and we can choose which one to treasure. The fact is that if we took the time to know who we are we would better understand who those "fringe people" are, as well. They have the same innate value as human beings as we do, and are a source of great love just as we are. They have the same kinds of complex reasons for their problems as we have for ours: genetics, family backgrounds, cultural influences, etc. Instead of judging them, we can give them compassion, and in so doing realize that we deserve the same.

Control can become a way of life if you believe that your happiness, self-worth, success, passion, relationships, etc. depend on it. You can spend time and energy trying to get to a point where everything (including yourself) is a certain way, thinking that then you will be able to relax and enjoy. You feel good or bad according to how closely situations conform to your expectations. In everybody's life, though, there is always something that is not going according to plan. The universe rarely conforms to our expectations. It's like trying to keep ten ducks in a row—invariably they wander! Life is unpredictable and basing anything on being able to control it is futile.

Control can become an obsession, though, when you believe that your happiness, self-worth, success, etc. depend on getting rid of one specific problem. You think that if you can control "it," (ie. drinking, weight, a bad job, etc.) then everything else in your life will fall into place. Control becomes your top priority, and consequently gives your problem life! That's why "white-knuckled sobriety" is not real recovery. It is just more obsession and more control based on your low self-esteem. Real recovery is based on high self-esteem gained by establishing an honest, loving, relationship with yourself—not by trading one obsession for another. Would you rather trade one prison cell for another or be completely free?

There are simply many things which you cannot control, no matter how hard you try. You have no control over others, the past, true impossibilities, nature, aging, and some situations. Codependents cannot change the behavior of their loved ones. A child of a dysfunctional family cannot undo the truth of an abused childhood. An alcoholic cannot change their biological response to alcohol. There's no controlling earthquakes or hurricanes. Father time is benevolent but persistent, and for all their ranting and raving, compulsive gamblers cannot run the race, kick field goals, or determine the roll of the dice. Do you have to feel bad about these unwanted realities, or is it possible to feel good even though you are at the mercy of things out of your control?

There also exists in your life things over which you *do* have control, but *which you may not be willing or ready to change.* Many of our problems fall into this category. We know we have the ability to do something about our situations. We think we should change, we wish we could change, but we don't; an, this gives us great fuel for the fire of low self-esteem. We now have proof that we are weak, shameful, rotten! Not only do we have our problem, but we are powerless to stop it. We become our own worst enemy, and we expend all our energy in the battle for control.

In every instance, acceptance will transcend control. When there is something that you don't like about yourself or your life, something that exists right at this moment, you have a choice between resisting or accepting its presence. Your choice will determine your experience. If you resist by hating it, dwelling on it, and obsessing about control, you give it life, feel bad about yourself, and remain stuck. If you accept it without your judgements and shame, you take away its power. Accepting something doesn't mean that you like or approve of it, only that you are willing to accept reality, and release your problem's hold on you and your hold on it. Then you are free to think clearly about what to do next. Your time and energy are not caught up in resistance but rather in taking constructive action.

You might fear that accepting your problem would remove your motivation to change. Paradoxically, the opposite is true, because acceptance allows you the freedom to love yourself, shortcomings and all. Getting down on yourself, trying to beat yourself into change, or hating yourself for not being ready yet, never makes anything positive happen. Accepting yourself takes the emphasis off control and puts it firmly where it belongs—on loving yourself.

Let's examine these ideas in the following hypothetical situations:

Situation A: A problem that cannot be controlled

Jackie's problem is that she is an incest victim. The abuse happened, and therefore cannot be controlled. It is possible, however, for Jackie to change her feelings about the abuse, and she has two options available to her:

Option 1: Resistance

Jackie wishes she had not been sexually abused by her father, and constantly relives the horror. She thinks that she should be able to put it behind her, and that she shouldn't be so controlled by something that happened years ago. If she could just forget it, everything would be fine. She ignores the stomach aches she has at night, her frequent angry outbursts, and general feelings of sadness. She blames herself and her father, often dwelling on the event instead of living in the moment. She hates her father but is not honest with him about her feelings. She wishes she wasn't so afraid of men, and doubts her ability to ever have a happy life. Nothing ever seems to change.

The outcome: Jackie feels bad and has low self-esteem.

Option 2: Acceptance

Jackie wishes she had not been sexually abused by her father, but accepts the fact that it happened, and is doing things to overcome its devastating effects on her life. In therapy and in conversations with family members, she has come to a better understanding of why it happened. She has discovered that her father had a frightening and lonely childhood, with a father who beat him regularly and a mother who looked the other way. Jackie knows that this does not justify his actions, but she also knows that it was not her fault. She did not provoke the abuse and could not have prevented it. She realizes that a lot of her problems are a result of her low opinion of herself due to that abuse, and now she is experiencing feelings of compassion for both her father and herself. Jackie chose to confront her father in order to release some of her guilt. She now has a more honest relationship with him, although not a close one. Her growing freedom from the problem is also giving her a healthier sexual identity, and is improving her relationships with men.

The outcome: Jackie feels good about herself.

Situation B: A problem that can be controlled

Juan's problem is that he is compulsive eater. Even though it is possible for Juan to change his eating behavior, there are three options available to him:

Option 1: Change

This is the most straightforward option because Juan knows that compulsive eating is something that he can change. What's more, he is willing to tackle it and the issues that perpetuate it. He both wants to and is able to change his behavior. He concentrates on feeling good about himself even though his looks are different than society's ideal. He is using the energy he spent controlling his food obsession in positive ways. He understands how and why he uses food, accepts what this has done to his life, and forgives himself. He practices mindful eating, and tries to differentiate between his emotional and physical cravings. He has developed a number of supportive, caring friendships, and wants to begin therapy or attend meetings of some kind. Juan's focus is on feeling good about himself and nurturing himself with healthier eating habits, but he is not necessarily going to diet—weight is not his main concern.

The outcome: Juan feels good about himself.

Option 2: Resistance

Juan is capable of change (stopping his compulsive eating), but he is not willing or ready to change at this time. His energy is poured into wishing things were different. He thinks that if he could get his eating under control, he would deserve nicer clothes, better relationships, and a happier life. When he is thin, he will relax and enjoy, but at the moment, he is on guard against his cravings. Sometimes the pressure is too much, and he eats to escape, feeling bad about himself for doing so. Then, he eats to escape those bad feelings. Juan is caught in a vicious cycle. He understands the negative consequences, but feels so bad about himself that change seems impossible. Juan is tired, unhappy, and stuck.

The outcome: Juan feels bad and has low self-esteem.

Option 3: Acceptance

Juan accepts that although he is able to change, he is just not ready to do so at this time. He accepts that he compulsively overeats, and affirms his self-worth in spite of it. He understands that compulsive overeating serves him, and is careful not to judge himself harshly for needing it sometimes. He devalues the behavior and values himself. He dresses nicely, takes care of himself, has good relationships, and tries not to waste energy by dwelling on this particular trait. He accepts that there are consequences to his food obsession, such as potential or realized health problems, and that there is a social prejudice against people who are overweight. Lately, Juan is eating less, and instead, is choosing to spend more time gardening, talking with friends, and reading.

The outcome: Juan feels good about himself.

Exercise:

Differentiate between what you can and cannot control.

1. Describe something negative in your life that you cannot control.

a. What might your experiences be if you resist the reality of the situation?
(See Situation A, Option 1, page 76.)

b. What might your experiences be if you accept the reality of the situation?
(See Situation A, Option 2, page 77.)

c. Repeat this affirmation:
"Even though _____ (your negative), I am still a worthwhile person who deserves to be _____ (happy, in love, etc.)."

2. Describe something negative in your life that you theoretically can control.

a. What might your experiences be if you change the situation?
(See Situation B, Option 1, page 77-78.)

b. What might your experiences be if you resist the situation?

(See Situation B, Option 2, page 78-79.)

c. What might your experiences be if you accept the situation?

(See Situation B, Option 3, page 79.)

d. Repeat one of these affirmations:

"I choose to change _____ (your negative) because I am a worthwhile person who deserves to be _____ (happy, in love, etc.).

"Even if I choose not to change _____ (your negative) at this time, I am still a worthwhile person who deserves to be _____ (happy, in love, etc.) and can choose to change later."

TOOL 14:

Feelings:
Are we having fun yet?

Most of us want to be happy. We seek happiness from jobs, relationships, bank accounts, college degrees, physical appearances, change, and elsewhere. We refer to this relentless search as "the pursuit of happiness," and it gets a lot of good press. So much so, that we are convinced that if we look hard and long enough, we will attain it.

What happens, though, when we reach our goals and don't feel the elation we thought we'd feel? What if we're in ecstasy for a couple of days, and then instead of feeling great joy, we actually feel empty or worse? What if it was the wrong goal for us? Sometimes, we pick ourselves up and go for the next goal, like another job, mate, diet, or income bracket. We look around and see what appears to make the next guy happy and try for that. The "next guy" might be our neighbor, or more than likely, a subtle image conveyed to us through the media that suggests happiness can be found in sitcom lifestyles, the ideals of retouched magazine photos, or in mass-produced items that are everywhere we turn.

Usually, though, when we don't experience the feelings of happiness, joy, peace, and well-being that we're after, we think something is wrong with us. This is the down side of the pursuit and false promises of happiness. We feel bad about ourselves because no matter what we do, we don't feel good enough. Not only is happiness out of our reach, but we are failures for not reaching it.

It is no wonder that we have problems. They protect us from this pain! It's no fun to feel bad, but the fact is that no one is always happy. There is a wide range of emotions, some positive (happiness, love, enthusiasm), some negative (guilt, fear, shame), and some fairly neutral (boredom, ambivalence, numbness). Feelings are a mixed bag, unless, of course, you are resisting feeling some of them by using your problem.

Our problems help us control our feelings by distorting, confusing, masking, and distilling them. For some people, the range of negative emotions are simply avoided no matter what they are. For others, feeling bad has payoffs of its own: to manipulate other people, as an excuse for poor performance, to keep people at a distance, or for attention. We might avoid feeling happy too, because we fear that it will give way to disaster. After a while, our problems make it almost impossible to distinguish exactly what we are feeling.

We think we need to control our feelings, just like we think we need to control ourselves. We don't trust them, they take us by surprise, they often get us in trouble, and we are afraid of them. We label feelings as "bad" or "good" and ourselves "bad" or "good" for having them. Few of us are taught that feelings are a legitimate, important part of life. We're not used to feeling or identifying them, and we have no experience expressing them in constructive ways. For these reasons, many of us have a history of denied, accumulated feelings with no outlet, nor do we know what to do with the feelings we have in the present. All we know is that we have to keep them in check because, like a dam holding back water, they have a power we know is overwhelming.

We don't realize the energy it takes to keep those feelings back, evidenced by illness, fatigue, and depression. Still, no matter how hard we resist them, feelings get through. If we have a compulsive problem, the quickest fix is to channel feelings through that. We feel better even thinking about escape. If we deny that the problem itself is out of control, we can go on indefinitely with these quick fixes; but, if we admit that our problem is not really helping, shame rises to the top of our list of painful feelings as soon as the temporary high wears off.

Shame is the most devastating of all feelings. It deserves special attention here, because it is the opposite of self-esteem. The two are mutually exclusive. Being ashamed of ourselves means that we believe something is fundamentally wrong with us, apart from merely having negative feelings. No matter where we picked up this notion, its effects on the rest of our lives is profound. If we believe ourselves to be innately bad, deserving of shame, then we will spend the rest of our lives trying to hide that fact and numb the pain of it.

In order to keep the secret of our shame, we lie, blame, manipulate, and withdraw from honest and intimate relationships, because we fear that the truth about us would disgust anyone who knew it. We don't want to face the shame, either. So, we cut ourselves off from the pain by hiding ourselves, our feelings, and our spontaneity. The ironic thing is that we think we are hiding our "real" self when the fact is that we are hiding a false one! We are not innately bad, we are innately good. That is our "real" self.

What's more, the knowledge of and connection to this goodness makes us willing to have all of the feelings that come along. When we love ourselves, we can feel anger, sadness, boredom, confusion, and jealousy; because, we know that these feelings do not change our worth at all. Our worth is not based on experiencing positive feelings like happiness or love, either—we are good regardless.

Here's some things to keep in mind about feelings:

Feelings exist.

Even if you don't recognize or understand them, you do have them, and are handling them in your own way. You might be storing them in your aches and pains, transferring them onto someone else, or denying that they exist. When you finally allow yourself to open up to them, you might have a deluge of feelings. Eventually, though, the flow will even out and you will learn to experience and appreciate all kinds of feelings.

Feelings are a mixed bag.

Once you begin to feel, you cannot pick and choose which feelings to have any more than you can pick and choose which events will occur in your life. Once you're on the roller coaster, you're on for the whole ride, ups and downs.

Feelings are legitimate.

They occur for valid reasons, and are important because they influence your subsequent choices. For example, if someone has treated you badly and you feel anger as a result, that is a natural way to feel. Your anger is a signal indicating that you need to take care of a situation, and the power behind it will help you do just that.

Feelings tell you something.

Feelings can be feedback about something that happened or is about to happen. Sometimes, they are the direct result of your belief system, thought patterns, or what you say. They can be physical and/or emotional reactions. If you can identify the cause of the feeling, you can better understand its message.

Feelings have power.

Feelings come in different strengths. Little ones can float right past, and big ones can bowl you over. Sometimes those big ones feel like the whole of us: we are fear, we are anger, we are love. We must remember at these times that we are not our feelings, we have our feelings. They have the power to transform our lives and others around us, but we have the power to transform them!

Feelings can mask other feelings.

Sometimes we use feelings to cope. Anxiety might be more acceptable than anger, hopelessness less painful than fear, and dissatisfaction a way to get attention or escape the challenge of responsibility. Stop and notice what you are feeling. Is there something else going on, too?

Feelings pass . . . if you don't resist them.

The best way to handle a feeling is to feel it, whether it is an old one or new. Feelings are part of life, and to resist them is to deny reality. Allow them to be without judging them, panicking, or necessarily taking any action. They might hurt, they might heal—you can't predict. Accept them for what they are—a natural human response. Feel them, connect them to their source if you can, communicate them if you need to, and then let them go.

Your feelings do not reflect your worth.

You are not your feelings, you *have* your feelings. You are not a good person because you feel good, nor are you a bad person because you feel bad. As I have said over and over, your worth is a given—it has nothing to do with how you feel.

Exercise:

Identify and express your feelings.

This exercise will help you to identify your feelings and develop creative options for expressing them. These new methods will be helpful for you, especially when you are tempted to use your problem as a substitute for feeling. Write down your answers, and repeat the process with other examples.

1. What is the predominant feeling you are having?
Example: anger

2. List words that more accurately describe what you are feeling.
frustrated, anxious, disappointed, embarrassed, hurt

3. Describe any specific event that may have triggered this feeling.
Mom called me "lazy and hopeless."

4. How might you commonly express this feeling in unsatisfying ways?
Eat a bag of cookies by myself. Sit around and mope. Kick the dog.

5. What are some other ways to express yourself?
Tell Mom that her words hurt me, and that I'm doing my best. Write Mom an angry letter and then decide whether or not to send it. Have a raging, screaming pillow fight with a good friend. Kick Mom, and pet the dog!

TOOL 15:

Think and speak positively.

Three men waited at a stop light to cross a busy street. When the light turned green, they stepped off the curb, and were nearly hit by a car swerving through the intersection. One man screamed at the driver, "You idiot, you practically killed me! I hope you crash into a wall and kill yourself." Then he thought, "I never should have walked on this stupid street. My heart's beating so fast, I'll probably have a heart attack." The second man thought, "Thank goodness that kind of car handles so well. I doubt if any other car could have swerved out of our way with such control. We're lucky, indeed." The third man was oblivious, and when asked his opinion, replied, "What car?"

Everyone has a different perception of reality. Our thoughts and reactions to events are never exactly the same as anyone else's, because we are each so unique. Our roots, experiences, and important influences are as different as our genetic codes. Even identical twins who are raised together process their worlds through different filters. The control center within us that determines our unique view of the world and ourselves is the mind.

The mind has irrepressible energy, working day and night, manifesting thoughts, dreams, and feelings. Sometimes we use it constructively, but usually we leave it on automatic pilot, allowing it to spin off in whatever direction it wants. When we are exhausted by its constant motion, we want to turn it off. We feel a need to turn it off just to get some peace and quiet. Some people do this with exercise or meditation, others with alcohol or drugs; but no matter what we do, it's only a matter of time before the mind begins churning again just as persistently as ever.

Most of our thoughts are habitual, honed by repeated patterns of thinking. Just as a river follows its course, wearing away at the earth deeper and deeper, our thoughts follow their course of least resistance with the same twists of logic and turns of preconception as they weave their way through our mind.

People with problems have thinking patterns which are not only habitual but distorted. They jump to conclusions without supporting evidence or they magnify the negatives and ignore the positives. They chronically compare themselves with others, dwelling on what "could" or "should" be. All of these distortions, and more, affect their recoveries in direct ways. For example, if they tend to think in all-or-nothing terms, then anything short of perfect recovery is the equivalent of failure. This obviously will sap their motivation! If they suppose everything that goes wrong is due to some defect within themselves, there will always be a reason to feel bad and turn to their problems.

We don't seem to realize the extent to which our minds influence our experiences. Every thought and word we express is a reflection and result of our predominant mental attitude. Every reaction that we have is processed through our mental filter. For this reason, it is not so much specific circumstances or events which create our realities but rather our interpretation of those circumstances and events. You can't change a horrible situation into a good one, but you can change how you think and feel about it. An example of this is how the late Orson Welles once reacted to a fire which destroyed many of his most treasured keepsakes. A talk show host asked him if he was pained by the disaster—a logical question. Surprisingly, Welles replied that the fire was wonderfully liberating, because it freed him of his attachment to those irreplaceable, hallowed possessions. Welles had a positive experience by seeing good in what most people would think of as a tragedy.

In recovery, you may think you only need to change your actions, but you also need to improve the nature of your thoughts. Recovery is like a clean-up process for the mind; we need to practice reprogramming it.

First, you need to focus on recovery instead of your problems. This is simple. The mind can only think one thought at a time, and whatever it focuses on is what exists for it at that moment. If you think about your problems, weakness, and shame, that's what you get. If you try to be cheerful, gently directing your mind towards a positive outlook, that's what you get. Since you experience what your mind thinks about, "Think lovely thoughts!"

Also, choose your words very carefully, because they have tremendous power. Words create our thoughts, and thoughts create our feelings. When you think, "I am worthless," you feel worthless. You don't even have to be aware of the words; they can exist subconsciously with the same effect. Likewise, the words we speak influence us. Therefore, to break habitual patterns of negative thinking, you have to consciously select and use different words. For example, try eliminating profanity from your vocabulary, especially when referring to yourself or your outlook on life. See the difference in your attitude when you rephrase from "I should recover," to "I choose to recover." The emphasis shifts the feelings from obligation (resentment, anger, powerlessness, etc.) to choice (creative, motivated, powerful, etc.). Even if it seems like a simple idea, you have to practice. Be persistent and consistent, rephrasing over and over until new, positive words and phrases become habitual.

Last, and most crucial, what we think influences our circumstances. What you thought in the past is in large part responsible for your present state of affairs, and what you think now will affect the future. As you gently direct your mind in a more positive direction, you start to see sides of situations which you previously would have missed. Perhaps there is an opportunity, a lesson, or simply a reason to be grateful. You begin to experience feelings of joy, fullness, and love. These feelings radiate and draw more goodness. Your experiences will eventually mirror your mental attitude.

Breaking your patterns of negative thinking takes practice. How easy would it be to redirect a river running downstream? You have to catch yourself in mid-sentence and reverse the flow of your words. You must make a conscious effort to think and speak positively. If you hear yourself saying, "I'm stupid," you need to add, "but I'm smart enough to correct my mistakes." Use the power of new words to counteract your programmed responses.

Your mind can be your enemy, or it can be your friend. It can create problems or can be a tool for achieving self-esteem. Your mind has been thinking in limited, habitual, and distorted ways; and you've believed it! You've been saying, "There is so much wrong with me." What good does that do? Besides, that's not true! The truth is that you are worthy just as you are whether you believe it or not. Your center of goodness exists whether or not you give it any notice. Even if your mind tries to convince you otherwise, repeat over and over again, "I am worthwhile. I am capable of great love. I am always doing the right thing, etc." Speak to yourself and of yourself with love and respect. This will manifest in your recovery.

Exercise:

Change your mind.

Stilling the mind and doing affirmations are two of the most powerful activities you can do to change habitual negative thinking.

1. Rest your mind. Sit or lie down for five to twenty minutes, and imagine something peaceful, such as a particular spot (the beach, a childhood haven), a scene (a field of flowers, a painting), or a feeling (love, warmth). If thoughts come up, observe them and allow them to pass. The more you practice this, the easier it gets. Don't try too hard, the point is to relax and quiet your mind.

2. Repeat affirmations, such as:
   - I trust myself.
   - I feel warm and loving toward myself.
   - I make the most of every day of my life.
   - I'm great!
   - (Make up more of your own!)

TOOL 16:

Face the truth about your family.

From the time we leave mother's womb and realize that we are separate, we search for our meanings and identities. Our families thus become our first and most influential teachers. We learn what love is and how to practice it. We learn about work, play, communication, intimacy, standards, and the consequences of mistakes. We learn all about life from our family's point of view, and feel a sense of belonging by doing things the way they do.

Families are systems, each member influencing every other in a delicate balance. What we learn from them is based on the relationships between the members, including ourselves; and it is within this system that the seeds of self-esteem are sewn. When our family treats its members with love and respect, we are encouraged to trust them and be ourselves in spite of mistakes, fears, doubts, ups, downs, and all. Under these nurturing circumstances, we learn that it is valuable as well as permissible to have the most important relationship of all, the one with our own selves.

People with problems often come from families where it is not okay to be one's self. This is generally true of overtly "dysfunctional families" of alcoholism, drug abuse, violence, etc., but can also be true of seemingly "normal" families. The relationships between members are based on unmet needs instead of unconditional love, and each learns to adjust in their own way. In extreme circumstances, it becomes a matter of emotional or physical survival for children to bury feelings, deny experiences, and put on an act. This is where the first tie with the self is severed.

In many cases, children ignore faults and rationalize abuses in order to preserve an idealized image of their family. It is too frightening to think that one's parents are horrible, neglectful people, so idealizing them is protection from these fears. Unfortunately, this lays the groundwork for a more harmful rationalization. In order to make sense of the fact that these same trusted caretakers are hurting them in any way, children must believe that they deserve what they get. To preserve blind admiration for their parents, they think of themselves as bad. Their minds protect them by lowering their self-esteem.

Your problem is a warning sign. You can't create an identity for the sake of your parents or in spite of them. You can't hold onto problems to keep from being washed away in the flood of a hurtful past. Those problems are not sufficient substitutes for parents who didn't love you the way you needed to be loved, or who couldn't be trusted to take care of your fragile self. You must face the truth about your family's influence on you, and build healthier relationships based on honesty and unconditional self-esteem.

Some families provide a framework which lowers self-esteem in the following ways:

• In order to make sense out of the way we were treated by our families, we rationalized that we deserved what we got. Even little incidents affected us. If we were ignored, we thought we were insignificant. If we were not given tasks to do, or what we did accomplish was not appreciated, we thought we were incompetent. If we always had to follow rules, we believed that we didn't know what was best for us. When we were afraid even though we were told not to be afraid, we thought we were wrong for having our feelings. In short, we assumed that our families were fine, and there was something wrong with us.

• Convinced that there was something wrong with us, we hid our shameful selves and put on an act. We adopted both positive and negative aspects of our parents' personalities in an effort to show them our love. Sometimes we developed these traits unconsciously, and in other cases, we wore them proudly. We even took on problems like theirs, as if our destinies were a given, "My father was a drunk, his father was a drunk, so I'm a drunk, too." If we were not openly rebellious, we tried to be invisible or keep the peace. Overall, we stayed on guard for external cues to show us how to act. We denied our spontaneity, repressed our feelings, or did whatever it took to insure our emotional and physical survival. In the process, we lost the relationship with ourselves.

• At some point, we believe that we are this act. The shame of being inherently bad is layered with so many years of pretending, that we define a new identity for ourselves. On the inside, though, there remains a gnawing empty place. Something is missing from our lives and we search for it in relationships of all kinds: friendships, mates, children, jobs, possessions, degrees, religions, *and problems.* Most of the time, we don't even know what we are looking for, although it is our own selves that we have lost.

• Seeing other family members also pretending strengthens our reliance on the act. It becomes "normal" not to be ourselves. Furthermore, since no one is communicating with each other, we are all alone—together. When they are being neglected or abused, we feel powerless. We may even feel bad when we are treated better. In either case, our self-esteem is lowered.

• At some level we are aware that we are kidding ourselves, and this, too, lowers our self-esteem. Even though we have learned the art of self-deception, which allows us to abuse ourselves through our problems, there is a little voice which notices and berates us. It sounds like our parents!

Facing the truth about your family will raise your self-esteem for the following reasons:

• Facing the truth gives you the opportunity to define for yourself what normal, loving behavior means. You can now parent yourself in your own style, to get the compassion, nurturing, encouragement, intimacy, trust, and other love that you missed as a child.

• It validates your experiences of the past and is a direct link to the self which you denied so long ago. By uncovering the illusion and facing the truth, you are saying in effect, "Yes, this is the way it really happened, and it hurt." You are affirming that your family's behavior had no bearing on your real worth. All along you had a place of love within that you failed to see.

• It validates your experience of the present and is another direct link to your real self. In this case, the truth affirms, "Yes, I am influenced by the past, and I still hurt. All along, I have been worthwhile and important, and now I am willing and able to esteem that place of love within me."

• It enables you to make a conscious decision about what you want to do about the truth. Each individual must make their own decision, unique to their personality and their ability. Do you want to confront your family or deal with the realizations by yourself or in therapy?

• It creates the possibility for having a healthy, honest relationship with your family. Exposing the truth to other family members might lead to confrontation. Some might fear that the family would shatter if the truth were told, while others may welcome exposing the illusions. In any case, bringing up the truth about old hurts would affect all family members. Everyone may not be capable of the honesty you desire and have worked towards in recovery. This could mean the end to the family relationships as you know them, but, on the other hand, it could lead to more meaningful ones based on mutual respect, hard emotional work, and the awareness of truth.

• It begins a process which may eventually lead to forgiveness. When the layers of hurt and resentment are stripped away, forgiveness is possible for some people. First, the truth must be told, and then the members involved must acknowledge and understand it. It is important that the rage and grief be worked through, because premature forgiveness can be a way of denying the full content of what happened, a way to avoid any more confrontation. True forgiveness is the last step—if it is taken at all, and it is a monumental one.

• Finally, acknowledging the truth enables you to see that your parents too might have been the victims of a troubled past. Parents cannot teach what they do not know, and chances are good that yours unknowingly passed their childhood legacy down to you. Many things besides bloodlines can be found on a family tree. What are some common characteristics of your parents, grandparents, brothers, and sisters? Tendencies towards substance abuse, eating disorders, or depression can be genetically inherited, but personality traits, values, types of relationships, how you treat others, problems, and solutions can also be found on your family tree. Draw one!

Have compassion for the child in you that is still feeling the pain of not being loved unconditionally. Express your hurt. Let the child speak! You might choose to confront your family or not. Perhaps they are not even living, yet their influence on you remains. You can still write them a letter or confront them with your feelings at their grave or before a photograph of them. Their response might be no more silent than if they were alive! However, the change will take place in you.

Exercise:

Remember the past to change your feelings.

Feelings of compassion and connection raise your self-esteem; feelings of resentment and blame lower it. This exercise is intended to help you reorganize your thinking patterns to change how you feel now. Although it is outlined around a family incident, you can use the same technique for other kinds of situations as well.

1. Remember a specific incident from your past, when you felt hurt by a parent.

   My father once kicked me when I was upset.

2. What happened just before the incident?

   His mother had died, and I was brooding.

3. Describe the incident and your thoughts and feelings at the time.

   My parents were sorting through my grandmother's possessions in her apartment, and I felt invisible, sad, worried, and afraid. I sat down on the floor in tears, and my father yelled at me, which made me cry even harder. Then he kicked me and left me there alone.

4. Imagine the situation as you wish it would have happened.

   I wish my parents would have comforted me.

5. Why didn't it happen that way?

   My Dad did not know how to express his grief or comfort me.

6. Treat your parent and yourself with compassion for that specific incident.

   I feel sorry for my father because I didn't understand his pain. I forgive him for kicking me, because his frustration and stress at that moment were beyond his control. I also feel sorry for that moment as a child, when I wasn't loved the way I needed to be loved.

TOOL 17:

Be aware of the media's message.

Marketers use the media to manipulate us, subtly lowering our self-esteem. People who rely on their problems for short-term fixes are especially susceptible to believing that what somebody has to sell, whether it is a product, a person, or a belief will better their lives. In a free-enterprise system, tremendous profits and power are had by people who exploit our insecurities, dreams, and need to feel good. While the pocketbook of any one of us is insignificant, the sum of our collective incomes has enormous potential to advertisers, the entertainment industry, and politicians. We are bombarded with media images that sell us products, services, values, concepts about ourselves, and elected officials, all based on the same kind of imaging. The more we are manipulated, the less confidence we have in our ability to make personal decisions. We have increased feelings of helplessness, futility, and inferiority; and our self-esteem gets lower and lower.

Obviously, the most dominant medium in our lives is television. It is our vehicle for entertainment and information. Seen and unseen forces use it to toy with our emotional well-being, spoon-feeding us happy families, super heroes, and larger-than-life protagonists. They define for us ideals different from our realities, to which we involuntarily compare ourselves. The more we watch, the less fulfilled we feel.

We are also inundated with advertising for expendable products that give us more of the same. The underlying message is that there is something basically wrong with us—if we buy what they are selling we will be happier, healthier, sexier, and better off. We learn to doubt that our teeth are clean enough, our hair the right shade, or our car as sexy as it should be. While this basic idea—that we are not okay as we are—damages our self-esteem, the cruelest blow comes after we buy into the products and beliefs and find that nothing about us has changed. Not only were we insufficient before, but we are so bad that nothing will help!

We ignore the fact that these idealized images themselves are not real. For a magazine advertisement's photo of a model, several hundred pictures are taken, set up in advance with perfect lighting and background. Only one is selected and then it is touched up! Wrinkles are removed, pores are airbrushed, and colors are brightened. (Of course, the time and expense spent on magazine ads is pennies compared to the amount spent on television commercials.) Obviously, the models from these ads don't look as picture-perfect as their photos. Nor are they as happy as the characters they portray. The sad truth is that these models have the same problems as everyone else, including eating disorders, for example, which some use to maintain a marketable look.

To add insult to our emotional injury, we know that some of the people in those advertisements are paid more for hawking a soft drink or pair of shoes than we will earn in a lifetime of hard work. The entertainers of today are our demigods. We worship them and what they appear to have. They're the highest paid members of our society, and regardless of what successes we achieve in our own occupations, we know we will never be on the same level as superstar athletes, musicians, or actors. Ironically, we relish any gossip that drags their "true" identities through the mud. We get a thrill to hear that a movie star is getting divorced or a football star is addicted to drugs, because— in a perverted kind of way—it makes us feel better to know that they're not so happy after all. This somehow settles the score but certainly does not make us feel any better about ourselves.

Television news also caters to our need for entertainment and can lower our self-esteem. On the surface, it seems like an objective, worthwhile service, which we can rely on to keep us in touch, but the truth is that most television news is just titillation to keep us hooked on commercials. Remember, news shows are primarily divisions of huge, profit-making, entertainment networks. Their first concern is business. The news comes in fifteen to thirty second bits, highlighted by human interest stories and tabloid journalism. If a movie star is sued for paternity and a country is invaded at its borders, you can be sure that the movie star will receive at least equal time. We like being amused, but at some level we are aware that we are being patronized by condescending reporting. Furthermore, when we allow ourselves to be informed of important topics or current events with such simplicity, we feel complacent, lazy, and guilty because we are choosing to be entertained rather than informed.

Most newspapers, magazines, and other sources of "infotainment" are not immune to criticism, either. For the most part, the news is condensed into brief summaries for quick reading to fulfill that audience's need to be informed without an investment of time. That way, they can read the important news in a few seconds and skip to the sports, comics, or fluff. Color photos, catchy graphics, and sensationalized stories keep readers turning the pages and seeing the advertisements. Again, this reminds us that we are small, not involved, and not okay the way we are.

There's more. In a healthy democracy, people need to take the time to be well-informed, interested, and assertive about their opinions. Unfortunately, in our society, we are withdrawing from this process as evidenced by the decreasing numbers of voters turning out each election day. It is apparent that we are giving up our power to imaging and our need to be entertained. The media intentionally or unintentionally conspires with our elected officials to broadcast their images in situations that have nothing to do with the issues. For example, we're force-fed a quick visual menu of the president playing softball and waving to reporters instead of hearing information that is relevant to our national and international well-being. In the end, we choose politicians based on three second smiles, paid advertising, entertainer endorsements, and buzz words; because, savvy campaigners or network programmers do not give us enough credit for wanting or being able to understand crucial political issues. No wonder we feel so helpless! No wonder our self-esteem is so low!

Surely, the media and individuals who use it are not all villains. Entertainment is an important, necessary part of our lives when not taken to the extreme. Also, television and the news media do, at times, provide information that is vital to us all. Advertisers have also campaigned against drug abuse, provided information about sexually transmitted diseases, and generated support for many worthwhile causes, in addition to other valuable contributions. Along these lines, entertainers are among the most active and generous philanthropists in our society; and, even though they are generally elected by fewer than half of the eligible voters, the majority of politicians responsibly represent their constituencies.

To avoid being manipulated by media images, raise your self-esteem. The most direct way to do this is by getting in touch with your own goodness, opinions, values, creativity, feelings, and experiences. Spend time with yourself. Certainly, we all have a legitimate need to relax and be entertained, but we must also understand how media marketing affects our already fragile self-esteem. Pay more attention to the hidden persuaders. Look through the hype. Transcend the power of the image!

Exercise:

Ten things-to-do to take power

Every individual can express and enhance their self-esteem through positive action. Asserting yourself makes you less susceptible to manipulation by marketers. You are affirming, "I can decide what is important to me. I care about myself and my world. I can make a difference."

Pick from this list of suggestions for things to do:

1. Realize how imaging directly relates to your problems and fight back! For example, if you have a food problem (such as compulsive eating or bulimia), look through magazines and newspapers ripping out advertisements, photos, and articles that promote your negative feelings about weight, body image, and food.

2. Be aware of the content of your entertainment. When you realize how you are being manipulated, you won't be so affected. Call or write those in charge to express your views. Television networks, for example, are sensitive to viewer feedback; let them know why you refuse to watch certain shows.

3. Become more aware of how television exploits your feelings. Notice how emotions like happiness, love, passion, and security are used as sales tools. Be more selective about what you watch, and turn off your television more!

4. Boycott products that offend you, and let the advertisers know that you will not buy from them and why. Rethink your buying habits. Advertisers spend more on promoting brand name recognition than they do on promoting individual products. If you reach for brand names without thinking, consider generic instead.

5. Find alternative sources for news. If most of your information comes from local shows or weekly magazines, consider other options, like public broadcasting radio and television, special interest groups' newsletters, and carefully selected newspapers.

6. Speak out on issues, contact lawmakers with your views, and work for politicians who have goals like yours.

7. Write letters to your favorite entertainers to encourage their support for projects you find worthwhile.

8. Be environmentally conscious. For example, learn more about the destruction of the world's rain forests and ozone layer, use less plastic, and recycle. You can also help others to recycle, such as neighbors who may be unable or uninterested in doing it on their own.

9. Get involved with local community projects which have a direct effect on you and the people nearest you. Donate your time and money. Find out about needy families that you may be able to help personally.

10. Copy this list and give to your friends. Post it on bulletin boards and refrigerators!

TOOL 18:

Keep good company.

Our problems are supported by the company we keep. I've talked about keeping the company of good thoughts, positive language, your inner voice, compassion, honesty, and other strong influences. I have not, however, mentioned the effect that good people can have on your recovery and self-esteem.

Face it, your drinking buddies are not going to urge you to get sober, but someone has to! Recovery is too tough to do without support. You must keep the company of people who believe in your strengths, value your uniqueness, allow for mistakes, have flexible expectations, and are open to communication. They make you feel good about yourself when you are with them. They make you feel less alone. They will give you reasons to continue.

Recovery inevitably means a change in your relationships. Sometimes this hurts. You must let go of people who are unable to support your changes. If your problem has been your best friend, you must find other friends. Even if your highest highs have been with your drinking buddies, you need to let them drink without you. It's okay to let go of friendships which don't further your recovery. You are better off without them. There is always the possibility that old relationships will undergo a transformation if both parties share in a willingness to change. Your priority, however, is keeping the company of those who enhance your self-esteem.

Professional therapy is an excellent way to take care of yourself. Perhaps you can't buy love, but you can pay for good company! In therapy, you are encouraged to value your own needs and practice honesty in a safe, intimate environment. It is a place to learn new ways to cope with your painful feelings. Along these lines, it is important that you find a type of therapy or therapist that is the best company for you. This may mean shopping around, but that's okay, too. It is your life, your self-esteem, your recovery.

Look for good company! Associate with other people in recovery. Go to support groups, and develop a network of friends who can relate to your experiences. Take classes on co-counseling and active listening techniques, attend lectures on self-improvement topics, hang out at recovery bookstores, churches, synagogues, or ashrams, where you will find seekers. However, be selective. You don't need a lot of friends, just good ones.

Be good company by showing compassion, sincerely listening, and reminding yourself of the goodness of the other person in the course of conversations. Instead of waiting for people to come up to you, be brave and say hello with a big smile and a cheerful attitude. You might be surprised how easy it is to influence them in a positive way by silently offering them your good wishes, turning them into good company, too!

The most important company you keep is your own. Practice being good company for yourself. Laugh. Buy a joke book, go to a comedy store, watch a funny movie, or just spend some time making goofy faces at yourself in the mirror. You do have your silly side, and so does life. Say, "Ha ha ha, hee hee hee, ho ho ho," over and over—really! Repeat that out loud five times and see what happens. See how you feel.

As you raise your self-esteem, you will begin to enjoy time alone, because you can experience strongly the love in your own heart. Spend quality time with yourself. Listen to music, visit museums, read uplifting books, do those things that you have always wanted to do. Talk with yourself out loud or by writing. Try looking at yourself in a mirror for five full minutes. Study yourself carefully, stare into your own eyes. Who is that? Try looking inside of yourself with your eyes closed. Get to know who you are.

Have relationships that nurture your emotional, physical, and spiritual growth. The right kinds of friends will help your recovery and raise your self-esteem. Remind yourself at all times, keep good company.

Exercise:

Consider the company you keep.

1. List five or ten people with whom you spend the most time.

2. Who supports your problem? How?

3. Are you willing to end any of these relationships?

4. Who is actively supportive in your recovery? How?

5. Whose company do you sincerely enjoy?

TOOL 19:

Practice love.

I'll be brief and to the point. Practicing love is the most important self-esteem tool for recovery, because when we practice love, we are making a connection with our real selves. This love cuts through the layers of false selves that we wear for protection, and makes clear that we are at our core, not flawed, but divine. We come in contact with our capacity for compassion, creativity, humor, goodness, and love. We realize that we are truly worthy of self-esteem.

Here are some ideas about love and how to practice it:

• The more we focus on love, whether giving or receiving, the more love exists in our life. When we practice it, it expands.

• Love is something everyone knows how to do instinctively, like breathing. Perhaps you think you've never experienced it, or have forgotten how; but anyone can learn to be loving. If you feel awkward practicing, be patient. You don't need to be perfect, just persistent.

• Love does not come from words, a lover's embrace, or parental approval. It comes from your own heart. Your problem has been a barrier, keeping love from getting in or out.

• You can't use up your love; you have an infinite supply. There is no need to limit love (I'm not talking about sex) to a single person, family, or friends. You can love everyone and everything: movie stars and old cars; teachers, preachers and double features. You get the idea!

• Love is a natural healer. If you have trouble believing this, read some books by Bernie Siegal, Leo Buscaglia, great spiritual teachers and philosophers, among others.

• Love is a choice. At every moment, you have that choice.

Inner Loving

• Self-love does not magically happen when all of your problems are eliminated. It happens when you unconditionally accept yourself for better or worse. It happens when you spend time with yourself instead of your problem, practicing and affirming your worth in all situations.

• Practice love assuming that you are a worthy and important person regardless of your past or problems. Do affirmations and visualizations to remind yourself of this.

• Listen to your inner voice. It is always there to guide you toward what is best for you. When you follow its lead, you are affirming that you want to do the right thing and trust your own judgement.

• Quiet your mind's constant chatter by taking a few minutes each day to meditate on your inner goodness. Your mind will resist, but with practice, you will be able to let the thoughts go and feel the connection to the source of love that is inside of you.

• Relaxation is a way of taking care of yourself. Get away from it all in healthy ways, like going out to dinner, watching a little television, going for a walk, doing yoga, using self-hypnosis or breathing awareness techniques, praying, and singing.

• Pamper yourself. Buy something that you have wanted for a long time. You are worth the money, time, and effort. Don't be afraid to be extravagant!

• Take care of your body regardless of your body type. It is worthy of great care. Give it good food, take relaxing baths or showers, get enough sleep and healthy exercise. Take a self-esteem bath!

• Put a picture of yourself, nicely framed, in a special spot normally reserved for pictures of people that you love. Put a flower in front of it. Honor yourself!

• Treat yourself respectfully, as if your words and deeds are those of a great being. It's true, you are!

Outer Loving

• Recovery means giving up the relationship with your problem and connecting with not only your inner self but the outer world as well. Love will emanate from you, and the universe will return that love back to you.

• Recognize love in the uniqueness of every person, works of art, music, literature, the innocence of small children, sunrises and sunsets, good deeds, laughter, etc. Stop to smell the roses! They are a sample of nature's loving essence. If you are looking for love, you are more likely to find it.

• Become a giving person. This is a wonderful way to open your heart and feel your own inner love. Give your time and energy. You can't feel bad about yourself when you're doing good deeds for others! Contact a local charity and volunteer. Visit a retirement home. Babysit for someone—me!

• Give affection. Give hugs. Pet your dog. Say hello to strangers in a cheerful way. Be affectionate in your attitude as well.

• Give compliments freely. This will enable you to receive them from others in the future! When someone gives you one, graciously accept it.

• People give and receive love in their own unique ways and to the best of their abilities. Practice understanding and compassion.

• Love has a way of transforming situations. Try approaching a difficulty with love and see what happens.

Don't simply read this list, do it!

Exercise:

Practice love.

Here are more specific things to do today and everyday:

1. Repeat this affirmation: "I honor the love within me."

2. Do this visualization: Sit or lie down comfortably in a quiet, peaceful place. Close your eyes, and take five long,

deep breaths, feeling your body relax more and more, breathing out tension and worries. Just let them go for now. Then, breathing naturally, focus on inhaling light and warmth. Fill your heart with this glow, and imagine it spreading through your whole body. It is a joyous, welcome feeling. When your heart feels as bright as the sun, allow this inner light to diffuse into the air around you. You are filled with and surrounded by love. Sit for as long as you want bathed in your feelings.

3. Tell someone you "love" them. This may feel scary, but it gets easier with practice, and it feels great to them and you!

TOOL 20:

Expect miracles.

Let me tell you about a seemingly insignificant event that transformed my life. After nine years of binge-eating and vomiting, my bulimia was more severe than ever. My father, who knew nothing of my eating disorder, invited me to accompany him on a trip to Bequia, a tiny island in the West Indies. For the five days we were there, my food problems magically disappeared as I enjoyed the beautiful weather and beaches, and learned a form of batik design from a native woman. On our last night there I had a dream, which I recorded in my journal the following morning, "I met a woman whose name was Gürze. She had mink hair and was inhabited by seven animals." I even drew a picture of her.

When I returned home, my obsessive eating resumed. Between binges, I created batik fabrics and made a five-foot doll of Gürze to model them. I brought the doll to a department store in New York City to sell the fabric, but everyone was more in love with Gürze!

On that trip I came across a magazine article on the binge-purge syndrome. It was one of the first articles ever written that perfectly described my eating disorder. Incredibly, the author of the article was conducting group therapy sessions minutes from my home. This was a miracle I could not ignore. With her help my recovery soon began.

Within a few months, my life changed dramatically. I moved to the West Coast, intensified my recovery, and began making soft-sculpture dolls full-time. In fact, my husband Leigh and I fell in love at first sight while I was selling dolls—not a minor miracle in itself. Gürze Designs became internationally well-known and were sold in more than 300 cities. I gradually quit my bulimia, writing and publishing the story of my recovery for Gürze Books.

For years I did not know what "Gürze" meant. As far as I knew it was just a name from a dream. Yet Gürze held special meaning for me. In her own way, she initiated my recovery, helped me meet my husband, and was the impetus for a successful soft-sculpture and publishing business. Gürze proved to me that I was a source of love and creativity. She was my own private miracle.

Seven years after I first met her in my dream and began to use her name, I met a student of Bavarian dialects who noticed my company letterhead and proclaimed with great certainty that "Gürze" was a familiar greeting amongst peasants in a remote region of Bavaria.

Its literal translation is, "Greet God" or "Hello, I see the God in you." This miraculous dream-name exactly conveyed what Gürze had meant to me!

Whether you realize it or not, each step towards loving yourself is an expression of what your inner heart desires. As you proceed in your recovery, you will notice that the universe wants to grant your wishes! *It wants you to love yourself, and it is showing you this through miracles.* The following quote by the late pianist Arthur Rubenstein, expresses these ideas:

"I have noticed through experience and through my own observations that Providence, Nature, God, or what I would call the Power of Creation seems to favor human beings who accept and love life unconditionally. And I am certainly one who does, with all my heart. So I have discovered as a result of what I can only call miracles that whenever my inner self desires something subconsciously, life will somehow grant it to me."*

We do subconsciously want to love ourselves. When we practice self-esteem we connect with that desire through the inner voice which is urging us to recover. This voice, this love in our hearts, has always been there, but our problems have separated us from it.

As we let go of our problems and are more willing and able to connect with this center of love, we realize that everyone has this same center. We are all connected by a common bond of inner greatness which wants to be known and is known when we enter into a loving relationship with ourselves. Remember, self-esteem is the means and it is the goal. Practice love, see love in others, and you will come to know the sweetness and joy of your very own self.

Expect miracles! Situations and events are designed for you to love yourself. The universe supports you and you are worthy of that support. Ask it for what you want now—recovery from your problems and high self-esteem. Maybe reading this book is one of your miracles. I hope so!

Exercise:

Wish upon a star.

1. Go outside to a safe place on a dark, clear night.

2. Lie on your back and effortlessly gaze up at the stars.

3. Look and wait. After fifteen or twenty minutes speak your thoughts:

   - Wish out loud for anything and everything you want.

   - State out loud your wishes for recovery.

   - Say words such as these: "Love has always been a part of me, and is my connection to the entire universe. I am the infinite source of love."

Notes

Tool 1
John Bradshaw: *Bradshaw: On the Family,* Deerfield
Beach, Florida: Health Communications, Inc., 1988.

Tool 2
Janet Jacobsen, "Killing the Pain," *Recoveries,* edited by
Lindsey Hall & Leigh Cohn, Carlsbad, California:
Gürze Books, 1987.

Tool 3
For more information about Pat Snyder or her association, contact her directly:
    Pat Snyder, Director;
    American Anorexia/Bulimia Assoc. of Philadelphia
    34th & Civic Center Boulevard
    Philadelphia, PA 19104
    (215)244-2225

Tool 6
Earnie Larsen, *Stage II Recovery,* New York: Harper &
Row, Publishers, 1985.

Charlie McMordie, "Silhouette of a Snowman,"
Recoveries, op. cit.

Tool 7
Lindsey Hall and Leigh Cohn, *BULIMIA: A Guide to
Recovery,* Carlsbad, California: Gürze Books, 1986.

Tool 8
Man in the Mirror, words and lyrics by Siedah Garrett
and Glen Ballard, ©1987 MJJ Productions Inc.

For more information about Robert Sundance or his
work, contact him directly:
  Robert Sundance, Executive Director
  Indian Alcoholism Commission of California, Inc.
  225 West 8th Street - Suite #910
  Los Angeles, CA 90014
  (213)622-3424

Tool 12
Matthew McKay and Patrick Fanning elaborate on this
idea in their excellent book *Self-Esteem,* Oakland, California: New Harbinger Publications, 1987.

Aldous Huxley, *Brave New World,* New York: Harper &
Row, 1932.

Tools 12 through 15
For more information about Marilyn Grosboll or her
work, contact her directly:
  Marilyn Grosboll, President
  Self-esteem Enterprises
  P.O. Box 1148
  Summerland, CA 93067
  (805)684-0787

Tool 20
Arthur Rubenstein, *My Young Years,* New York: Knopf,
1973.

About the Authors

In 1980, Lindsey Hall and her husband, Leigh Cohn, wrote a booklet about her recovery from the binge-purge syndrome. *Eat Without Fear* was the first publication solely about bulimia, and a few years later was revised into the book, *BULIMIA: A Guide to Recovery*.

Shortly after the release of Lindsey's story, she was the first bulimic to appear on national television. In the decade that followed, Lindsey and Leigh spoke about bulimia and self-esteem throughout the United States, wrote more books and articles on recovery topics, and consulted with sufferers and families of eating disorders and treatment professionals. Their works have been used in thousands of colleges, high schools, hospitals, and by professional therapists throughout the world. The tenth anniversary of her story was marked by the Bantam Books paperback *Eating Without Fear*.

Lindsey graduated from Stanford University with a degree in Psychology, and Leigh earned an M.A.T. in English Education from Northwestern University. They edit "The Gürze Bookshelf Catalogue" which includes a comprehensive selection of materials on eating disorders and related recovery topics.

Lindsey and Leigh are happily married and have two sons, Neil and Charlie. They feel fortunate that their projects help people become more self-fulfilled and loving.

Also written or edited by Hall & Cohn:

The Gürze Bookshelf Catalogue (FREE)
This comprehensive collection of books and tapes includes titles on eating disorders, recovery topics, dysfunctional families, self-esteem, and more.

BULIMIA: A Guide to Recovery
This superb guidebook offers a complete understanding of bulimia and a plan for recovery. It includes a two-week program to stop bingeing, insight from 217 recovered bulimics, things-to-do instead of bingeing, a guide for support groups, specific advice for loved ones, and "Eat Without Fear," Lindsey Hall's story of self-cure which has inspired thousands of other bulimics.

Recoveries: True Stories by People Who Conquered Addictions and Compulsions
Seven authors describe their own experiences in addiction and recovery from alcoholism, anorexia nervosa, bulimia, cigarette smoking, cocaine, narcotics, and suicide.

Dear Kids of Alcoholics
This is an honest, helpful, hopeful book for children (ages 8-17) of an alcoholic parent. Young readers will identify with the feelings of its main character, Jason, a boy who explains facts about alcoholism with touching stories about his dad's sensitivity to alcohol, destructive behavior, and recovery process.

FULL LIVES
Imagine being at a dinner party with sixteen extraordinary women who have overcome food and weight obsessions as they discuss: food, love, and intimacy; eating disorders: a great teacher; women united for social change; hunger and the inner-self; sexual abuse and eating; and being recovered and fat.

Order Form

The Gürze Bookshelf Catalogue (Do not add shipping below.)		FREE
Self-Esteem Tools for Recovery $10.95 5 or more copies $8.95 each		
BULIMIA: A Guide to Recovery $12.95 5 or more copies $9.95 each		
Understanding Bulimia-audiotape $11.95 5 or more copies $9.95 each		
FULL LIVES $12.95 5 or more copies $10.95 each		
RECOVERIES $9.95 5 or more copies $7.95 each		
Dear Kids of Alcoholics $8.95 5 or more copies $6.95 each		
Subtotal - - - - - - - - - - - - - -		
Tax (7% Calif. residents only)		
Shipping - - - - - - - - - - - - - - - 1 item: $1.95 / 2-4 $.95 each / 5+ $.75 each		
TOTAL * * * * * * * * * *		

Unconditional guarantee!
Be sure to include your name and address!

Phone orders to: (619)434-7533 -or-
Enclose payment (or institutional PO#) to:

Gürze Books
P.O. Box 2238
Carlsbad, CA 92018